Southern
BREADS

Southern BREADS

RECIPES, STORIES and TRADITIONS

MARILYN MARKEL and CHRIS HOLADAY

Foreword by Bill Smith

AMERICAN PALATE

Published by American Palate
A Division of The History Press
Charleston, SC
www.historypress.net

Photos by Chris Holaday unless otherwise credited.

p. 50: Recipe copyright © 2011 by Sheri Castle, from *The New Southern Garden Cookbook: Enjoying the Best From Homegrown Gardens, Farmers' Markets, Roadside Stands, and CSA Farm Boxes*. Used by express written permission from the author; p. 47: Recipe copyright © 1993 by Nathalie Dupree, from *Nathalie Dupree's Southern Memories*. Used by express written permission from the author; p. 28: Recipe copyright © 2012 by Nathalie Dupree, from *Mastering the Art of Southern Cooking* by Nathalie Dupree and Cynthia Graubert. Used by express written permission from the author; pp. 54 and 78: Recipe copyrights Darryl Williams, from his blog "From the Family Table" (fromthefamilytable.com). Used by express written permission from the author; p. 76: Recipe copyright Ricky Moore. Used by express written permission from the author.

First published 2016

Manufactured in the United States

ISBN 978.1.46713.744.7

Library of Congress Control Number: 2016948309

The authors sweep away many mythologies about Southern food and bread with an authoritative pen, making what follows a clear guide to mastering the mystical. Sit down and read it first, or at least the first few pages, to learn all the basics before proceeding. From there, imagine master instructor Marilyn is by your side, holding your hand, and move on fearlessly to baking your favorite bread. With her many years of teaching, she is able to anticipate missteps and lead the way to perfection. There are some wonderful toppings, as well, that are treasures to keep on hand or give away.
—*Nathalie Dupree*

CONTENTS

Traditional Southern cornbread, cooked in a well-seasoned, Tennessee-made Lodge cast-iron skillet.

FOREWORD

I was raised by a lot of good cooks. That was very useful to me in my career, though I didn't realize at the time what I was learning because I didn't cook with them; I just watched. But I suspect it was probably the most important thing to my profession, better than any training. Cooking, especially cooking bread, is such a part of everyday life.

The first cooking job I had was at the Carolina Coffee Shop in Chapel Hill in 1969, and I was the guy who made the rolls. We made yeast rolls from scratch in those days, and I loved doing that. The restaurant was famous for its rolls, giant and puffy—they were huge. And with the scraps we made cinnamon rolls, which they served for breakfast. Those were very famous, and they were ridiculous—as big as a dinner plate. We just saved all the scraps and rolled them out and added butter and nutmeg and sugar and so on and rolled them up. That was my first real cooking experience, and I hadn't thought about it again until just now, at least not in the context of the importance of bread.

There is huge fight that goes on constantly about sugar or no sugar in cornbread, depending on where you are from. It's an ongoing saga. People don't seem to be as combative about biscuits. There are many acceptable styles, and some are for breakfast and some go on top of cobblers; some are little and some are huge. I think people are more accepting of variations in biscuits than they are with variations in cornbread. The cornbread we make at Crook's has sugar and flour, which are bones of contention, but I do like other kinds, I have to say. We had a friend of mine in the restaurant from Louisiana as a guest, and he made skillet cornbread. It had no butter but oil instead. He actually flipped it like pancakes, and it was delicious. I'd never seen that done before.

Some barbecue places make what's called hot-water cornbread. It's hot water and lard and cornmeal, period. You start it on top of the stove and finish it in the oven.

It's very thin and chewy and common in eastern North Carolina and elsewhere. There's a poet named Patricia Smith who wrote a wonderful poem about hot-water cornbread called "When the Burning Begins." It's one of my favorite poems.

So breads, with all their many variations and traditions and memories, will always be a deeply important part of the culture of the South.

BILL SMITH

For more than two decades, Bill Smith has been the chef at Chapel Hill, North Carolina's iconic Crook's Corner, an establishment honored as a James Beard America's Classic Restaurant in 2011. Smith is also the author of two cookbooks and twice has been a finalist for the Best Chef: Southeast award from the James Beard Foundation.

ACKNOWLEDGEMENTS

For their help, the authors would like to thank Nellie Dee Wims (Grannie Wims), who made this book possible; Nathalie Dupree; Sheri Castle; Ricky Moore; William and Dianne Brinkley; Bill Smith; Susan Frankenberg; Bartow Culp; Wes Flanary; Darryl Williams; Willard Doxey; Dennis Hermanson; Tricia Collis; Cindy Dunlow; Alice Seelye; Betty Jane Holaday; Louise Henegar; Larry Flanary; Craig Gilbert; Glenda Flanary; Margaret Dodson; Tori Reid; and Jimmy Holcomb. We especially thank our respective spouses, Jim Markel and Sue Holaday, for putting up with us as we worked on this book. Last, but certainly not least, we thank Banks Smither at The History Press for his guidance and support of this project and his colleague Julia Turner for her amazing attention to detail.

Chapter 1
INTRODUCTION

When people are asked what defines the South, their answers will vary from differences in history, geography, climate and even accent. Perhaps the most important difference, however, is food. The South has many famous foods, but the most culturally pervasive and important is bread. The story of Southern breads is an extremely interesting one that helps us define who we are as a regional people.

Many regions of the world have their distinctive bread cultures: France has the croissant and baguette; Italy, the ciabatta and focaccia; the Middle East, pita; India, naan; and so on. In the South, we have cornbread, hushpuppies and biscuits. To a Southerner, these three breads are not just a side dish; they are essential to the meals they are served with. In fact, they are often the star of the meal: biscuits for breakfast (filled with jams, ham and cheese or just butter), hushpuppies as the required companion to barbecue pork and fried fish and cornbread at any time of the day. And it doesn't stop there; there are also numerous derivatives, such as spoon bread, zucchini bread, pumpkin bread and more, all uniquely flavored by the harvests of the South.

While these breads can be quite delicious absolutely plain, what goes on the bread can be equally important. Toppings and accompaniments allow the same bread to be eaten numerous days in a row but in a new way each time (example: cornbread panzanella and cornbread with pinto beans start with the same cornbread recipe, but the end results are quite different). Recipes can be turned into creations both sweet and savory.

Another important part of Southern bread is the stories that go with them. These led us to incorporate the bread memories of Southerners from across the region. Almost everyone has powerful memories of bread—of eating it or of watching it being made by a beloved family member in the kitchen. When asked, some responded first with "I don't have a good story," but after we got them thinking and talking, inevitably an important memory, often from childhood, soon came out.

The historical origins of Southern breads are also important, so we have assembled recipes from some of the earliest cookbooks to focus on the region's cuisine. Some may seem strange and foreign to us today, but others are not so different. Regardless, it is on these historical recipes that Southern bread culture has been built.

In cultures around the world, breads are a staple part of almost every diet. They are hearty and sustaining; there is a reason the idiom "staff of life," used in reference to bread, came into being in seventeenth-century England. Said American poet Emily Dickinson in a letter to a friend in 1845, "I am going to learn to make bread to-morrow. So you may imagine me with my sleeves rolled up, mixing Flour, Milk, Saleratus, & C., with a deal of grace. I advise you if you don't know how to make the staff of life to learn with dispatch." We heartily recommend the same to you.

Chapter 2
LESSONS TO LEARN

Before anyone can appreciate and understand Southern bread, they need brief lessons in three other important subjects: history, geography and science. Yes, this is still a cookbook, but it is also a tale that involves human migration, wars, slavery, airborne fungus, chemical reactions and scientists. It didn't start with our great-grandmothers in the kitchen with cast-iron skillets, after all.

Like many stories, this one begins far from where it has ended. Actually, we shouldn't say ended because the story of Southern bread is very much alive and still being written. But it all probably began in ancient Egypt. No one knows for sure, but we will give credit to the Egyptians for discovering how yeast works and baking the first leavened bread. The exact date is unknown, but it was probably over three thousand years ago. Before that, primitive forms of breads—essentially grains and other plants ground on a rock, mixed with water and baked on a flat stone—were common in many cultures.

WHEAT AND CORN

Wheat is a grass that originated in the eastern Mediterranean sometime after the last ice age. As people discovered the importance of the plant's grains, or seeds, as a foodstuff, it spread to North Africa and Europe. In the early 1500s, the Spanish brought it with them as a crop when they began to settle the New World. It did not grow in tropical climates, but in drier parts of the colonies, it did thrive. From it, breads were produced to feed colonists in the manner in which they had been used to in Europe.

Wheat eventually spread into the colonies of North America. It was certainly grown in the South but not in the quantities it was north of the Mason-Dixon line or later west of the Mississippi. In the South, cash crops like cotton and tobacco took prevalence

Above: An 1863 drawing by Edwin Forbes shows farm workers stacking wheat near Culpeper Courthouse, Virginia. *Courtesy Library of Congress.*

Left: Known by the scientific name *Zea mays*, corn, or maize as it is often called, is a native of North America. Its kernels, when dried and ground, are one of the bases of Southern bread culture. *Public domain.*

in fields. Up north, however, food crops were the choice of most farmers. So when the Civil War erupted, the South was at a disadvantage when it came to feeding troops due to a lack of—you guessed it—bread.

While wheat was an old-world crop, the other main component in the breads of the South originated on the same side of the Atlantic. Corn, or maize, is a grain plant native to North America that was first domesticated by the indigenous people of Mexico several thousand years ago. Like wheat, it began to spread through trade as its importance as a foodstuff was discovered. By the time the Europeans arrived, it was a staple food for the Native Americans they came in contact with across the New World. Settlers soon learned to make bread from corn the way the Native Americans had. Before the spread of wheat, cornbread was the most prominent bread product of the South. People ate it every day and with every meal.

In the South, corn was more common and more easily grown than wheat. Wheat was used in biscuits, which are, of course, a quintessential Southern food, but they were mainly saved for Sunday dinners and special occasions. At least, that was true in the early years before improved transportation and the great wheat fields of the plains states. Like wheat, corn is today often identified with other parts of the country. Midwest states Iowa and Illinois are the top producers by far, but cornbread remains perhaps the most Southern of all foods.

BLENDING CULTURES

As we've mentioned, the story of Southern bread begins in several places. Wheat-based bread came from the other side of the Atlantic while bread made with corn had it beginnings on this side. Several factors then played a role in the spread of bread and other foods. The first one is the movement of people. Just like you might borrow the recipe of a neighbor, the instructions for cooking were shared. When people moved or migrated they took recipes with them and continued to make them in the way they had as a way of holding on to comforting traditions of native lands.

That brings us to another factor: environment. Recipes that traveled to new lands often had to be adapted to available ingredients. If you were a colonist in Savannah, say, it was probably easier to purchase the staples necessary for cooking. If you moved inland to frontier areas, however, they might be more difficult (or expensive) to find. Wheat doesn't easily grow everywhere, for example, so that's how settlers first incorporated the traditions of Native Americans into their cooking.

Settlers also originated in many different places, and each had its own cooking traditions. When the British arrived, they continued to cook like they had in their home country. It was the same with the Africans, Spanish, Germans and everyone else. And in the New World, those traditions began to mix. In most of the South, the food began to reflect the traditions of the British Isles mixed with those of African slaves. In Louisiana, it was the French and the Africans. And in Texas, the influences of Spain and then Mexico became apparent in the food.

When people from these different cultures met, they were exposed to new tastes—and sometime they really liked these new tastes. So maybe a person from Alabama moved to Texas in the nineteenth century. They were making cornbread their way at home, but maybe in Texas, someone introduced them to jalapeño peppers, which are common in Mexican cuisine. The Alabama native might think,

"Hmm, these would taste good in my cornbread." Purely hypothetical, but you get the idea. So even within the South, breads are different depending on local traditions and influences. Hushpuppies are not the same everywhere, even differing in the same state, and making a biscuit in Virginia is not the same as it is in Texas.

Mentioning cornbread, it evolved differently in the northern United States. There, a type of the bread is made with sugar as a common additive. It is also usually made with ground yellow corn. In the South, white corn has always been more popular and adding sugar is a controversial topic. Said Mark Twain in his autobiography, "The North thinks it knows how to make cornbread, but this is gross superstition."

LEAVENING

Before all the traditions, before all handed-down and shared recipes, cooking is science. It is the reaction of various ingredients to one another and how together they produce delicious food. And in bread, the most important ingredients are the leavening agents.

The story of leavening, or rising, in bread begins with a fungus: yeast. Naturally occurring, this single-cell organism comes in hundreds of species. Some are bad for people, and some we probably couldn't live without. In baking, when yeast is added to dough, it essentially eats the naturally occurring sugars. In this process, known as fermentation, the waste product is the gas carbon dioxide. The gas forms bubbles, and as they rise, the dough expands. Adding sugar boosts the yeast's metabolic action even further.

Another product of yeast fermentation is ethanol alcohol. It plays a role in some types of bread, but without our yeasty friends, we wouldn't have beer, wine and liquor. In the production of those beverages, as yeast eats the sugars in grains and grapes, ethanol is the desired product instead of carbon dioxide.

Not that any cook ever needs to remember it, but the yeast strain almost always used in baking is *Saccharomyces cerevisiae*. It is commonly called by a name much easier to pronounce: baker's yeast. It is available in three types: fresh, active-dry and instant. A couple of other important facts: yeast doesn't like cold or heat, they go dormant below 40 degrees and they die in temperatures over 140 degrees Fahrenheit. Salt also controls the activity of yeast and can slow it.

Yeast occurs naturally in the air (it was perhaps discovered when some settled onto a forgotten bowl of porridge or something), and it is easy to make with a starter such as potatoes. In 1868, however, the first commercially produced yeast, Fleishmann's, made its appearance. Commercial yeast made it easier and quicker to have consistent results when cooking.

But all leavening is not done naturally, and that's where the scientists come in. For bread to rise, it still needs to "bubble." The answer was sodium bicarbonate, a

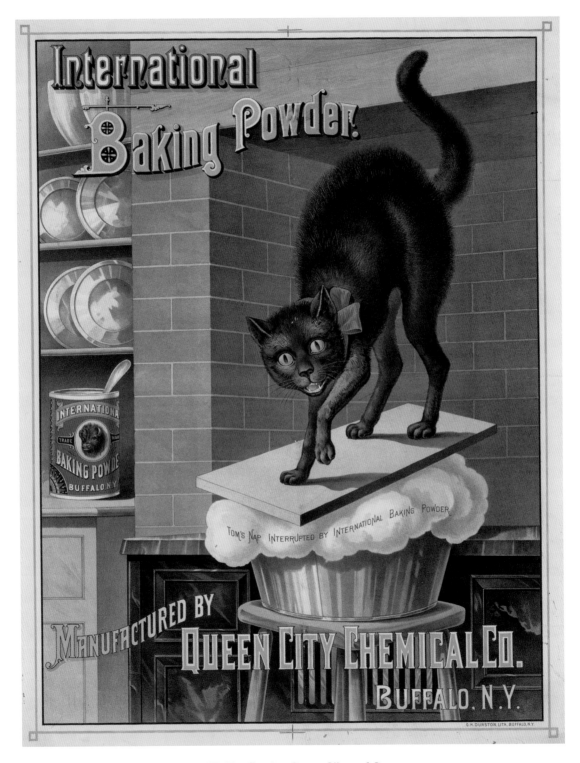

An 1885 advertisement for International Baking Powder. *Courtesy Library of Congress.*

chemical compound that worked like yeast but was quicker (hence the term "quick breads"). When mixed with acids in dough, it reacts to release carbon dioxide, causing bubbles and, in turn, rising dough. This happens slowly at room temperature, but when heated, dough rises much quicker.

Sodium carbonate, which is an alkali salt, has numerous applications. It is used in everything from toothpaste to laundry detergent and lubricants. Sodium bicarbonate ($NaHCO_3$) used in baking is a form that contains twice as much carbonate, giving it the prefix "bi." (Interestingly, sodium bicarbonate is also commonly used in fire extinguishers.)

As to how sodium carbonate came about, several people in different parts of the world take credit for the discovery or refinement of the process. In the late 1700s, the French Academy of Sciences offered a prize for someone who could produce soda ash (another name for sodium carbonate) from salt. The award went to surgeon Nicholas Leblanc in 1791. Though his process eventually proved to be economically infeasible, he essentially set the ball rolling. Half a century later, it was picked up by Belgian chemist Ernest Solvay; he gets most of the credit for modernizing the process in the early 1860s.

When sodium bicarbonate is mixed with a weak acid, the result is what is known as baking powder. When this substance reacts to water or heat, its acid controls when the bubbles are released. Rumford Baking Powder, called a double-acting powder, contains monocalcium phosphate as its leavening acid to react with the sodium bicarbonate. This acid releases two-thirds of its bubbles within a few minutes of mixing at room temperature. The last third of the bubbles (and more rising) occurs when heated in the oven. Rumford was one of several brands, including Calumet and Clabber Girl, introduced in the late 1800s that offered the same benefits to bakers.

Before Rumford, invented by American scientist Eben Horsford, baking powder had contained sodium bicarbonate and cream of tartar. Some cooks still swear by cream of tartar. Not creamy at all, it is actually a fine white powder with the real name of potassium bitartrate ($KC_4H_5O_6$). A naturally occurring byproduct of the wine industry, the name comes from the Greek *tartaron*, an encrustation on a wine cask.

Like sodium carbonate, cream of tartar has a long history involving European scientists. The modern process for manufacturing it was developed by the Swedish chemist Carl Wilhelm Scheele in 1769. Later, in 1832, the many physical properties of cream of tartar were discovered by French scientist Jean-Baptiste Biot. Coincidentally, Biot was awarded the Rumford Medal in 1840, a prestigious award established by Benjamin Thompson, Count Rumford. A science professorship was also named after Rumford at Harvard University. That position was held by Eben Horsford, who named his new company Rumford Chemical Works after his teaching position. That company's most famous product is Rumford Baking Powder.

It was other Frenchmen, however, who made the use of cream or tartar popular in cooking. In addition to its use in baking, cream of tartar had many other useful properties, such as helping to stabilize whipped cream and egg whites. Famed Southern chef Edna Lewis always preferred to make her own baking powder and mixed two parts cream of tartar with one part baking soda. We'll end our little science lesson with a fun fact: cream of tartar is a key ingredient in another kind of "dough"—Play-Doh.

So, now it's time to bake bread. But first a couple of ingredient basics:

Self-Rising versus All-Purpose Flour: Self-rising flour has leavening agents already in the flour while all-purpose flour does not. If a recipe calls for self-rising flour and you do not have that on hand, you can add 1 teaspoon baking powder and ¼ teaspoon salt for each cup of all-purpose flour.

Salt: There are so many options for salt on the market. These recipes are written for kosher salt, which is coarser than iodized salt. If you do use iodized fine salt or fine sea salt, just cut the amount in half. Says Marilyn, "I use kosher salt 95 percent of the time. I use a sprinkling of high-end sea salts occasionally, since they are terrific as a finishing salt (like on summer tomatoes)."

Chapter 3

BISCUITS

B iscuits have long been a rite of passage for aspiring cooks in the South. Many youngsters learned to make these fluffy and versatile culinary staples by watching older family members in the kitchen. Cherished recipes were often passed down in oral tradition without ever actually being written out.

While styles (drop versus rolled and cut) and procedures vary, most cooks agree on several important factors. First is the flour. Everyone has a favorite brand they swear by (Marilyn usually uses White Lily or Old Mill of Guilford), but the type of flour makes a big difference when making biscuits. Most in the South prefer brands that use summer soft flour instead of those that use winter hard flour. They feel winter hard wheat has too much gluten-forming protein to make a soft biscuit.

Secondly, most biscuit doughs are wetter than folks anticipate, but flour incorporated during kneading makes them manageable. Another important factor is the fat added to the dough. Butter makes biscuits dense while shortening makes them fluffier. Of course, good old-fashioned lard is the best…

There are so many options for biscuits. They can be served plain, with butter, with butter and jelly, with cheese, with sausage—the list goes on and on. That is actually one of the wonderful things about many Southern breads—all of the toppings and accompaniments. We've included many recipes for some favorite toppings, both sweet and savory, that will allow cooks to find something to match any taste or meal.

MARILYN'S BISCUITS

I'm sure my grandmother's biscuits inspired me to pursue a culinary career. When I was a child—maybe five or six—we visited her in Tennessee from where we lived in Georgia. Somehow, I would make myself intentionally wake up (though the smell of cooking bacon or ham usually helped) around 5:00 a.m. That would give me two hours just to be with her in the kitchen, sitting on a stool watching or helping when I got older. It was an old kitchen in an old house, and she would open the oven between batches to keep it warm.

Before she stopped cooking at age ninety, Grannie Wims had amassed eighty years of experience in the kitchen making biscuits and plenty of other Southern staples and delicacies. Asked (at age ninety-six) when she learned to make biscuits, she said the skill was passed down by her mother—the usual way—at age nine. I also asked what was her fondest memory of biscuit making and was surprised it was the same as mine—Christmas biscuits. Her house was always the place to gather for breakfast, and Christmas was particularly special. Once, when we had driven from our home in Texas to hers in Nashville for Christmas, my husband counted that she made 110 biscuits, in batches of 10, that Christmas morning. She wanted everyone to have warm biscuits when they came to breakfast.

I also was curious what Grannie Wims would say was her favorite biscuit topping. The answer: pear preserves. My grandfather, on the other hand, loved sorghum mixed with butter on his biscuits.

She had another remembrance of milk day. Once a week, her father would take his horse-drawn wagon and pick up the big cans. The first thing her mother did was take the cream off the top and save it. Then a lot of the milk would be churned to make butter or buttermilk, which was used in cooking biscuits and plenty of other things.

While on the subject of biscuits, my grandmother also shared a family story that went back even further. She said her grandfather (John Robbins) was wounded in the Civil War while serving in Chattanooga. From her home in Gladesville, over one hundred miles away, his wife, Temperance Ann, traveled on horseback to get him and bring him home. And what was the only food she was able to take with her and eventually share with her husband? Biscuits.

—Marilyn Markel

Serves 8

2 cups self-rising flour

¼ teaspoon baking soda

½ teaspoon salt

1 tablespoon sugar

4 tablespoons shortening

1¼ cups buttermilk

1 cup extra flour, any kind

4 tablespoons butter, melted (or more!)

Preheat the oven to 450 degrees.

In a medium bowl, combine self-rising flour, baking soda, salt and sugar. Stir with a pastry blender. Using your fingers or a pastry blender, add in the shortening until it is completely incorporated and the mix looks like coarse cornmeal.

Stir in the buttermilk. The dough will be very wet. Put the 1 cup extra flour in a small bowl and whisk lightly. Flour a small (2 tablespoons or 1 ounce) scoop or two spoons. Scoop a small biscuit-sized lump of wet dough and drop it into the extra bowl of flour.

Be sure flour is completely around each biscuit and shape the biscuits with your hands in the flour into a soft round in the size of a sea scallop. Dust off excess flour and pack the shaped biscuits tightly into a buttered 8-inch round pan or skillet. Dip the spoons or scoop into the flour before proceeding with each scoop of biscuit dough.

Brush the biscuit tops generously with the melted butter and place in the oven. Bake about 20 to 25 minutes, or until lightly browned. Brush liberally with butter and turn them out onto a cutting board or heat-proof surface. Serve hot.

From this worn Fiesta bowl, given to her when she was married, Marilyn's Grannie Wims produced an estimated 300,000 biscuits.

WILLARD'S BISCUITS

Willard Doxey and Marilyn taught biscuit classes together for ten years.

Breakfast, lunch and dinner, biscuits were just something I grew up with. My mother and my grandmother both made them all the time. It was an everyday food we all took for granted. Biscuits may be simple and basic, but they are intimidating to people who haven't cooked. It's really all about practice. The class Marilyn and I taught together for years really helped people understand and enjoy more, and that was a good thing. Marilyn and I also have different styles, so our class let people identify with whichever version they grew up with.

—Willard Doxey

Makes 12 or so 2½-inch biscuits

3 cups soft white flour
1 heaping tablespoon baking powder
½ teaspoon baking soda
1 teaspoon salt
1 teaspoon sugar
12 tablespoons cold shortening, cubed
1⅓ cups cold buttermilk
softened butter

Preheat oven to 450 degrees.

Sift dry ingredients with a pastry blender in a large bowl. Cut in cold shortening until completely incorporated and the mixture resembles coarse meal.

Stir in buttermilk with a spatula until a loose ball forms. Do not overmix.

Turn onto a floured board and knead 4 times, turning 90 degrees each time. Add flour to the surface and board as needed.

Pat into a circle ¾-inch thick and cut with a well-floured 2½-inch sharp cutter, or whatever sized biscuits you prefer. Dip the cutter into flour after cutting each biscuit. Cut the biscuits as closely as possible to use all the dough possible from the first batch. Gather scraps, knead a couple of times and cut again.

Place biscuits close, but not touching, on a parchment-lined sheet pan.

Bake for 15 minutes, or until nicely browned on the top and bottom, turning the pan halfway through baking.

Brush with soft butter and serve immediately.

———•◆•———

NATHALIE DUPREE'S TWO-INGREDIENT BISCUITS

One of the legendary figures of Southern cuisine, Charleston's Nathalie Dupree has won four James Beard Awards, is the author of more than a dozen cookbooks and has hosted more than three hundred television shows. Also a good friend of Marilyn's, the two have worked together to teach many cooking classes.

Makes 14–18 2-inch biscuits

2¼ cups self-rising flour
1¼ cups heavy cream
melted butter, for brushing

Preheat oven to 450 degrees.

Select the baking pan by determining if a soft or crisp exterior is desired. For soft exterior, use an 8- or 9-inch cake pan, a pizza pan or an ovenproof skillet where the biscuits will nestle together snuggly, creating a soft exterior while baking. For a crisp exterior, select a baking sheet or other baking pan where the biscuits can be placed wider apart, allowing the air to circulate and create a crisper exterior. Brush selected pan with butter or oil.

Fork-sift or whisk 2 cups of the flour in a large bowl, preferably wider than it is deep, and set aside the remaining ¼ cup. Make a deep hollow in the center of the flour with the back of your hand. Slowly, but steadily stir 1 cup of cream, reserving ¼ cup of cream, into the hollow with a rubber spatula or large metal spoon, using broad circular strokes to quickly pull the flour into the cream. Mix just until the flour is moistened and the sticky dough begins to pull away from the sides of the bowl. If there is some flour remaining on the bottom and sides of the bowl, stir in just enough of the reserved cream, to incorporate the remaining flour into the soggy, wettish dough. If the dough is too wet, use more flour when shaping.

Lightly sprinkle a plastic sheet, a board or another clean surface with some of the reserved flour. Turn the dough out onto the board and sprinkle the top of the dough lightly with flour if sticky. With floured hands, fold the dough in half and pat it into a ⅓- to ½-inch-thick round, using a little additional flour, if needed. Flour again if sticky and fold the dough in half a second time. If the dough is still clumpy, pat and fold a third time. Pat the dough into a ½-inch-thick round for

normal biscuits, a ¾-inch round for tall biscuits or a 1-inch-round for giant biscuits. Brush off any visible flour from the top. For each biscuit, dip a 2-inch biscuit cutter into the reserved flour and cut out the biscuits, starting at the outside edge and cutting very close together, being careful not to twist the cutter. The scraps may be combined to make additional biscuits, although they will be tougher.

Using a metal spatula, if necessary, move the biscuits to the pan or baking sheet. Bake the biscuits on the top rack of the oven for a total of 10 to 14 minutes, until light golden brown. After 6 minutes, rotate the pan in the oven so the front of the pan is now turned to the back, and check to see if the bottoms are browning too quickly. If so, slide another baking pan underneath to add insulation and retard the browning. Continue baking another 4 to 8 minutes, until the biscuits are a light golden brown. When they are done, remove from the oven and lightly brush the tops with softened or melted butter. Turn the biscuits out upside down on a plate and cool slightly. Serve hot, right side up.

BLUE CHEESE BISCUITS WITH PEACH CHUTNEY

This is basically a variation on Willard's biscuits, and the cheese can be changed to suit your preference. Not a fan of blue cheese? No problem. You can substitute most medium-textured cheeses. We made it with Somerdale Red Dragon Mustard Seed and Ale cheese, and it was delicious. You may also follow the directions for your favorite biscuit mix and add the blue cheese when rolling the dough or add mild herbs, such as chives, parsley or dill. Let your creativity shine and create your own version.

Makes 20–24 1½-inch biscuits

3 cups soft white flour
1 heaping tablespoon baking powder
½ teaspoon baking soda
1 teaspoon salt
1 teaspoon sugar
12 tablespoons cold shortening, cubed
¼ pound finely crumbled blue cheese, plus a little extra for putting inside the biscuit
1⅓ cups cold buttermilk
softened butter
peach chutney, for serving
prosciutto-style country ham, for serving

Heat oven to 450 degrees.

Sift dry ingredients with a pastry blender in a large bowl. Cut in cold shortening until completely incorporated and the mixture resembles coarse meal. With a spatula stir in grated or finely crumbled cheese.

Stir in buttermilk with a spatula until a loose ball forms.

Turn onto a floured board and knead 4 times, turning 90 degrees each time. Add flour to the surface and board as needed.

Pat into a circle ¾ inch thick and cut with a well-floured 1½-inch sharp cutter, or whatever sized biscuits you prefer. Dip the cutter into flour after cutting each biscuit. Cut the biscuits as closely as possible to use all the dough possible from the first batch. Gather scraps, knead a couple of times and cut again.

Bake for 10 to 12 minutes, or until nicely browned on the top and bottom, turning the pan halfway through baking.

Brush with soft butter and serve immediately with peach chutney and country ham.

PEACH CHUTNEY

Peaches may be the ultimate Southern fruit. This is the perfect summertime creation that can be enjoyed fresh or all year long when canned.

Makes about 12 half-pint jars

2 cups sugar

2 cups cider vinegar

6 pounds sliced peaches (about 12 large peaches)

2 large cloves garlic, peeled and minced

2 tablespoons fresh peeled and grated ginger root

¼ cup finely chopped onion

2 tablespoons salt

⅓ cup crystallized ginger

⅓ cup currants or raisins

zest of 1 lime

2 to 4 small jalapeño peppers, seeded and minced

Be sure the pot size is large enough to comfortably hold all ingredients with ¾ of the top of the pot still visible. Over medium-high heat in a large, nonreactive pot bring sugar and vinegar to a boil. Reduce heat to medium, and once the sugar dissolves, add all other remaining ingredients. Cook for about I to I½ hours (or until thick). Stir often.

Remove from heat and skim off foam.

Ladle into sterile jars leaving a ¼ inch of headspace. Clean rims with a clean, damp cloth and add lids.

My mother taught school, so she really only cooked on the weekends. Then, though, she cooked big, and she liked to have company. One of her specialties was cheese biscuits, and everyone who came to dinner expected them. She used a lot of cheese, sharp cheddar, and cut out the dough with a special juice glass that was just the right size.

They were best on Sunday morning. We split the biscuits and toasted them and put butter on them. I liked to add jelly, too, even though they were cheese biscuits, but that may have been just me.

—Betty Jane Holaday

BACON GREASE BISCUITS WITH SORGHUM APPLE BUTTER

Sorghum, similar to molasses, is made from the stalks of a grass with high sugar content. Used as a sweetener in the South since before the Civil War, it is not as common as it once was due to the availability of sugar cane. Combined with apple butter, a slow-cooked applesauce especially popular in the Appalachian South, it creates a unique, rather old-fashioned taste.

Makes I2 2½-inch biscuits

Biscuits

3 cups soft white flour

1 heaping tablespoon baking powder

½ teaspoon baking soda

1 teaspoon salt

1 teaspoon sugar

8 tablespoons cold butter, cubed

4 tablespoons bacon grease

1⅓ cups cold buttermilk

softened butter

Sorghum Apple Butter

3 pounds tart apples

½ cup sugar

1 tablespoon apple pie spice

½ cup sorghum

Biscuits

Heat oven to 450 degrees.

Sift dry ingredients with a pastry blender in a large bowl. Cut in cold butter and bacon grease until they are completely incorporated and the mixture resembles coarse meal.

Stir in buttermilk with a spatula until a loose ball forms. The mixture will be wet.

Turn onto a floured board and knead 4 times, turning 90 degrees each time. Add flour to the surface and board as needed.

Pat into a circle ¾ inch thick and cut with a well-floured 2½-inch sharp cutter, or whatever sized biscuits you prefer. Dip the cutter into flour after cutting each biscuit. Cut the biscuits as closely as possible to use all the dough possible from the first batch. Gather scraps, knead a couple of times and cut again.

Place biscuits close, but not touching, on a parchment lined sheet pan.

Bake for 15 minutes, or until nicely browned on the top and bottom, turning the pan halfway through baking.

Brush with soft butter and serve immediately.

Apple Butter

Peel and seed apples. Cut into 1-inch chunks. Add sugar and apple spice and cook on medium heat until dark but still chunky, about 25 minutes. Stir the sorghum into the applesauce.

My father never ate a meal without a fork in one hand and a biscuit in the other. Oh, and Virginia Gaddis, who lived up the street, she loved butterbean biscuits. Try it, it's delicious. Us kids, we used to make fun of her, but one day, we said we're just going to try it. So we all loved it, especially if it had a little corn in it. Butterbean and corn biscuits, mmm, that's good. And tomato with butter on a biscuit—oh, my goodness. My first husband introduced me to butter and tomato on a biscuit. And that's very, very good.

—Alice Seelye

SAUSAGE AND BISCUIT PINWHEELS

My mother always made these on Christmas morning when we were growing up. We always added a smear of grape jelly. Muscadine butter, featuring a native Southern grape, is made by blending strained muscadine juice and pureed skins. Cooked for about an hour; it will take on the texture of butter. It lets you put a twist on that classic sausage biscuit with common grape jelly, which is usually made with Concord grapes, a crop from "up north."

—Marilyn Markel

Makes about 20 pinwheels

1 pound breakfast sausage
1 batch biscuit dough, recipe follows
melted butter
muscadine butter or grape jelly

In between 2 layers of plastic wrap, roll sausage into an 8 by 12 rectangle.

On a floured surface roll out biscuit dough into a 9 by 13 rectangle. Turn frequently to ensure it is not sticking. You may want to split the dough and sausage in half to roll.

Remove plastic wrap from the top of the sausage, leaving wrap on the bottom. Turn upside down and press sausage directly onto dough. Cover the dough almost completely with the sausage, leaving only a ½ inch uncovered on each side. Then remove the remaining plastic wrap. Starting at a 13-inch edge, roll the dough into a pinwheel. Dampen the outer edge with a little water and pinch closed with your fingers.

Chill for 1 hour.

Preheat oven to 425 degrees.

Cut chilled dough at 1-inch intervals. Place sliced pinwheels on parchment-lined sheet pan and brush with melted butter. Bake for about 10 to 12 minutes, until biscuits and sausage are cooked through. Brush with butter and serve with grape jelly or muscadine butter.

BISCUIT DOUGH
2 cups soft wheat flour
2 teaspoons baking powder
¼ teaspoon baking soda
½ teaspoon salt
½ teaspoon sugar
8 tablespoons butter, cut into 1-inch cubes
⅔ cup buttermilk

Sift dry ingredients with a pastry blender in a large bowl. Cut in cold butter until completely incorporated and the mixture resembles coarse meal.

Stir in buttermilk with a spatula until a loose ball forms. Do not overmix.

Turn onto a floured board and knead 4 times, turning 90 degrees each time. Add flour to the surface and board as needed.

Wrap in plastic wrap and refrigerate until ready to use.

When I was a child we had help to do the cooking when my mother and father were at work. Her name was Bridie Greer. Making biscuits was kind of her thing, so she didn't really let us help. We did love to watch, though, because she would give us pieces of dough to play with. We would make little twisty things or snakes or maybe tie knots and then Bridie would bake them.

Well, the first year I was married—you can imagine what kind of cook I was—we lived in a little apartment, and I was working. For dinner, I used to make those canned biscuits that were popular and kind of new. One time, I decided to make some from scratch and served

them to my husband for dinner. "Is this a new kind of biscuits?" he asked. "Yes," I told him. "Well, don't get that kind anymore." I figured I better get serious after that! So finally, after some searching and refinement I learned to make biscuits that live up to expectations."
—Margaret Dodson

PLUM RUM JAM

Makes 5½ pint jars

8 large, unpeeled red plums, pits removed and chopped
4 cups sugar
¼ cup lemon juice
1 pouch liquid pectin
2 tablespoons rum

Put the plums in a large saucepan and crush with a potato masher. Add the sugar and lemon juice and bring to a boil, stirring often.

Boil for 1 minute, stirring constantly. Add pectin and rum and remove from heat. Skim off foam.

Ladle into sterile jars leaving a ¼ inch of headspace. Clean rims with a clean, damp cloth and add lids. Refrigerate when cool or process in a hot-water canning bath.

CRABAPPLE JELLY

Yield 8–10 half-pint jars

4 pounds crabapples
4 cups water

4 cups sugar
1 pouch liquid pectin

Place fruit and water in a saucepan and bring to a boil. Reduce heat and simmer for an hour or so, until fruit is soft, stirring frequently.

Strain through a double layer of cheesecloth.

Measure 4 cups of the crabapple juice and sugar into a clean saucepan. Bring to a boil over medium-high heat, stirring often. Cook until jelly coats the back of the spoon.

Boil for 1 minute, stirring constantly. Add pectin and remove from heat. Skim off foam.

Ladle into sterile jars, leaving a ¼ inch of headspace. Clean rims with a clean, damp cloth and add lids.

Pack into hot sterile jars. Refrigerate until using or process in a hot-water bath.

All the young'uns growing up in the rural northeastern North Carolina community called Ross, knew that my grandma always had biscuits cooked and ready for the taking in her red-and-white kitchen cupboard.

My grandma lived just two houses away from me and a dozen of my first cousins also lived within shouting distance of Grandma's. Whether we were out playing baseball in her backyard or having a Hopscotch game in her swept-clean front yard, the best snack was a cold biscuit from Grandma's kitchen. Sometimes, you hit the jackpot when you would sneak in for that precious cold snack. Grandma had made chocolate gravy, a sweet Hershey's cocoa concoction that was found hardening in an old tin pot sitting on the table beside the stove. Those hardened flakes of sweet chocolate scraped off that pot and put on that cold biscuit made the best snack of my childhood.

—Tricia Collis

GRANNIE WIMS'S SAUSAGE GRAVY

This is my favorite biscuit topping. It creates one of those aromas that strongly reminds me of Grannie's house and would awaken me in the wee hours. Long cooking the crispy sausage tenderizes the meat and makes it homogenous, like a thick sauce. Additional milk (maybe a lot) is required for the slow cooking. Keep thinning so it does not stick or scorch.

—Marilyn Markel

Serves 6

1 pound breakfast sausage
2 tablespoons reserved fat
2 tablespoons flour
2 cups milk, plus more for slow cooking
freshly ground pepper, to taste

Cook sausage in a skillet over medium heat, crumbling into small pieces until *very* crisp. Drain sausage completely through a sieve and wipe out pan.

Return 2 tablespoons of reserved fat to the pan and place on medium heat. Reserve excess fat for another use or cool to room temperature and discard. Add flour and cook, stirring constantly with a whisk until the mixture is a tan color, about 5 to 10 minutes.

Add cold milk and whisk constantly until smooth and thickened.

Return sausage to pan and gently cook, stirring frequently over medium heat until thick. You may need to add more milk as the gravy thickens. The longer it cooks (up to an hour), the more the sausage becomes tender. Serve with piping-hot biscuits.

RED-EYE GRAVY

Looking for a way to use leftover coffee? Put it in your frying pan and make this Southern classic.

—Marilyn Markel

2 tablespoons butter

1—8 ounces good-quality bone-in country ham steak

1 cup coffee

2 tablespoons brown sugar

1 tablespoon molasses (or a little more brown sugar)

pepper, to taste

Heat butter in skillet over medium heat. Add country ham steak and sear well on both sides until nicely browned, about 5 minutes per side. Remove from pan.

Add coffee, brown sugar and molasses and bring to a simmer. Simmer until reduced slightly. Season with pepper to taste.

Slice ham pieces and serve with biscuits and gravy.

When I got married in 1949, I had no knowledge of cooking any meals because my mother did it all. She didn't make me learn; she tried but I wasn't interested. So when I got married, Louis was a coal miner, and when he'd come in, what he liked to eat was biscuits, gravy and

Louise Henegar, of Appalachia, Virginia, in the kitchen making biscuits. *Photo by Wes Flanary.*

the whole deal. First time I attempted it for him, he wouldn't eat them. It hurt my feelings, but I went on making them. Finally, I got to where I could make good biscuits just by trial and error. After a little while, I got as good as my mother, so he liked my biscuits. He had them every day in the morning when he came in from the third shift.

Making the biscuits, I just do it by eye. Imagine the amount of flour you would want for twelve biscuits. If I need to go more, I can. Add about an egg size of Crisco—we used lard back then—and buttermilk. You need a big bowl so you can move it around and knead it. The key is the kneading. Sometimes people don't knead enough and the biscuit falls apart; Louis hated the biscuits that fell apart. You have to learn the texture when you handle it in your hand. I can tell if it's correct by just feeling it in my hand. Then I just pinch them off—I don't roll them out—and put them in the oven.

—*Louise Henegar*

HONEY BUTTER

A warm biscuit right out of the oven with butter and honey on it—can there really be anything better?

—Marilyn Markel

Makes ½ cup

1 stick butter, softened to room temperature
¼ cup local honey
½ teaspoon kosher salt

Combine all ingredients.

PIMENTO CHEESE BISCUITS

In the South, pimento cheese has a lore all its own. Just like for biscuits, some will swear it should be made one way while others will vehemently argue otherwise. However you make it, it deliciously pairs with biscuit and is our favorite savory way to serve them.

—Marilyn Markel

Makes 12 2-inch biscuits

2 cups soft all-purpose flour
2 teaspoons sugar
4 teaspoons baking powder
½ teaspoon salt

½ teaspoon cream of tartar

½ cup shortening

⅔ cup shredded cheddar cheese

2 tablespoons minced chives

2 tablespoons finely minced drained pimento peppers, dried

⅔ cup milk

2 tablespoons melted butter

pimento cheese, recipe follows

Preheat oven to 450 degrees.

   Sift dry ingredients with a pastry blender in a large bowl. Cut in cold shortening until it is completely incorporated and the mixture resembles coarse meal. Add the grated cheese, chives and pimentos and stir with a spatula.

Stir in milk and mix until just combined. Do not overmix.

Turn dough onto a floured board and knead 4 to 5 times, turning 90 degrees each time. Add flour to the surface and board as needed.

Pat into a circle ¾ inch thick and cut with a well-floured 2-inch sharp cutter, or whatever sized biscuits you prefer. Dip the cutter into flour after cutting each biscuit. Cut the biscuits as closely as possible to use all the dough you can from the first batch. Gather scraps, knead a couple of times and cut again.

Place biscuits close, but not touching, on a parchment-lined sheet pan.

Bake for 15 minutes, or until nicely browned on the top and bottom, turning the pan halfway through baking.

Brush with soft butter and serve with pimento cheese.

SOUTHERN PIMENTO CHEESE

Serves 6–8

½ pound sharp cheddar cheese, grated

4 ounces pimentos, drained, dried and minced

2 tablespoons sweet pickle relish

¼ cup mayonnaise

salt and pepper, to taste

Combine all ingredients. Season with salt and pepper.

> My earliest memory is of standing on a chair in my grandma Sally's kitchen in Bertie County, North Carolina, and watching her make biscuits. She used a big wooden tray to mix the ingredients—my aunt still has it. I remember the flour sifter and the buttermilk and the lard. She rolled the biscuits out and cut them with a jar (my sister makes good biscuits still, but she uses the drop method). The kids couldn't roll, but we got the scraps after the biscuits were cut. We took them and laid them out on the old, thin blackened baking pan in curvy shapes. We called them snake biscuits and we loved them.
>
> —Cindy Dunlow

THE ULTIMATE BLT

Who said the BLT has to be served on white bread only? And if you've never tried any of the heirloom varieties of tomatoes that can be found at any farmers' market, you're in for a tasty treat.

—Marilyn Markel

There's just something about the combination of tomatoes and mayonnaise. You can buy it in a jar, but fresh mayonnaise is easy to make. Shown here with a vintage Wesson Oil mayonnaise maker.

Serves 6

12 large biscuits
2 heirloom tomatoes, such as Cherokee purples, green Cherokees or pink German Johnsons
8 slices candied bacon, recipe follows
¼ cup mayonnaise, or homemade mayonnaise, see page 120
salt and pepper, to taste

Slice biscuits in half. Slice tomatoes into biscuit-sized pieces. Cut bacon into 2-inch pieces. Spread 1 side of biscuit with mayonnaise, add a piece or two of bacon, a few slices of tomato and season with salt and pepper. Top with other biscuit half. Hold together with a toothpick and serve on a platter.

———•••———

CANDIED BACON

Serves 6

8 thick slices bacon
¼ cup pecan praline syrup or maple syrup
½ teaspoon cayenne
¼ cup light brown sugar

Preheat oven to 350 degrees. Place bacon on a rack set over a sheet pan. Line the sheet pan with foil to make clean up easier. Brush 1 side with syrup.

Combine cayenne with brown sugar. Liberally sprinkle onto the bacon. Turn bacon to the other side and repeat. Bake for 20 minutes, or until the bacon reaches desired crispness. Let cool.

I knew my grandfather and grandmother as very old people. My grandmother still controlled the whole house and the kitchen, but my grandfather was retired. He had time to go fishing with me or just sit on the porch, and he always had time for a smile.

Grandmother was all work. She was a proper and hardworking woman who looked mean to me, but she

wasn't. Grandmother got up before we did and baked biscuits and did the ham and eggs and whatever else there was. It was early in the '50s so she didn't have an electric stove; she had a wood-fired stove that loaded the wood on the left side, and the hot skillets were right over that. And the oven was on the other side of a wall from the fire, which made it bake. The men got the wood ready and brought it into the kitchen.

She got the fresh eggs from the chickens, and flour was from the local mill. So we got up to the smell of biscuits every morning. I liked to put butter and syrup figs onto the hot biscuits. That was my favorite.

—Dennis Hermanson

RAY'S CHICKEN-N-DUMPLINGS

From *Nathalie Dupree's* Southern Memories.

Serves 8

1 3-pound frying chicken
2 quarts water
1 onion, quartered
1 carrot, quartered
1 celery stalk, quartered
1 bay leaf
10 peppercorns
2 teaspoons salt
1 sprig thyme

FOR THE DUMPLINGS
3 cups all-purpose flour
½ teaspoon baking soda
½ teaspoon salt
5 tablespoons shortening
¼ cup chicken stock
⅔ cup buttermilk
1 tablespoon chopped fresh thyme
salt and pepper, to taste

Place the chicken in a heavy 5-quart stockpot with water to cover. Add the onions, carrot, celery, bay leaf, peppercorns, salt and thyme. Bring to a boil and then lower to a simmer. Gently cook 1 to 1½ hours, skimming any fat that may rise to the top.

Remove the chicken from the stockpot. When slightly cooled, remove the meat from the bones and reserve. Return the skin and bones to the stockpot and simmer 1 hour longer. Strain the stock, discarding the solids. Return the stock to the stockpot. Skim off as much of the fat as possible.

To make the dumplings, combine the flour, baking soda and salt. Lightly cut in the shortening until the flour resembles coarse meal. Add the ¼ cup chicken stock, buttermilk and thyme and stir to make a stiff dough. Turn the dough onto a lightly floured surface and knead gently 5 to 6 times. Pat the dough into a round, cover with plastic wrap and chill for 1 hour.

Making biscuits for dinner on cornshucking day at Fred Wilkins's home near Tally Ho, Granville County, North Carolina, in September 1939. *Photo by Marion Post Wolcott, Courtesy Library of Congress.*

Bring the strained stock to a simmer. Roll the chilled dough out to an ⅛-inch-thick round on a lightly floured surface, moving the dough after each roll to make sure it doesn't stick to the surface. Cut the dough into 4- by 1-inch pieces and drop them, one at a time, into the simmering stock, stirring often so the dough doesn't stick together. Cook gently 10 to 12 minutes, until the dumplings are firm yet tender. Add the reserved chicken meat to the pot and serve at once. Season with lots of salt and freshly ground pepper.

SHERI CASTLE'S SWEET POTATO BISCUITS

These biscuits are from my dear friend Sheri Castle. I have had the privilege to work with and watch Sheri teach classes over the years. She is one of the finest cooking instructors I know and passionate about Southern culinary heritage.

—Marilyn Markel

These biscuits are very tender and a little sweet, much like a good cream scone. Unlike most biscuits, they are better served the next day at room temperature. The night's rest makes them less crumbly and gives the flavors time to meld. They are a welcome addition to any fall or winter meal, particularly around the holidays. They make incredible ham biscuits. If you use a 1½-inch cutter, little ham biscuits are a crowd-pleasing hors d'oeuvre or buffet dish.

—Sheri Castle

Makes 15 2½-inch or 12 3-inch biscuits

2½ cups all-purpose flour, plus extra for rolling

1 tablespoon baking powder

1 teaspoon fine sea salt

¼ cup light brown sugar

¾ teaspoon ground cinnamon

½ teaspoon ground ginger

½ teaspoon ground allspice

½ teaspoon mace

½ cup vegetable shortening

1 cup roasted sweet potato puree

1 cup heavy cream

Preheat the oven to 350 degrees. Line a baking sheet with parchment paper or a silicone baking mat.

Mix together the flour, baking powder, salt, brown sugar, cinnamon, ginger, allspice and mace in a large bowl. Use a pastry blender or your fingertips to work in the shortening until the mixture is crumbly. Stir in the sweet potato puree with a fork. Slowly add the cream and stir until the dough comes together and pulls in all of the dry ingredients. Add more cream, 1 tablespoon at a time, if needed.

Pour the dough onto a lightly floured surface and gently knead until smooth and supple, about 8 turns. Roll or pat the dough to a ¾-inch thickness. Cut out the biscuits with a round cookie cutter. If the dough sticks, dip the cutter into some flour. Push the cutter straight down without twisting so that the biscuits can rise to their full potential. Place the biscuits on the prepared baking sheet.

Bake until the biscuits are firm and spring back when lightly touched on top, about 15 minutes for 1½-inch biscuits, 20 minutes for 2½-inch biscuits and 25 minutes for 3-inch biscuits. Transfer to a wire rack to cool to room temperature. Store at room temperature overnight in an airtight container before serving.

My grandmother lived in a little town in Edgefield County, South Carolina, and she was a fabulous Southern cook. Her name was Margaret Hunter Browne, but everyone called her Miss Hunter. When the grandchildren were visiting, she would make biscuits once a day. She swore by Adluh flour—it seemed like there was always an open bag of it in the kitchen—and, of course, always used buttermilk. I remember her rolling [the biscuits] out on a broken piece of marble and the rolling pin she used was actually a big pickle jar that she would fill with ice water. To cut the biscuits out, she used an old tin can that had once held Rumford baking powder.

When she finished cutting the biscuits, my grandmother would always take the leftover bits and bake them right at the end. Sometimes shaped like little rings of dough, they were sort of reverse biscuits. The grandkids loved those, and we would fight over them.

The biscuits were baked very fast and close together (she always said if you baked them separated the edges would get hard), and they came out of the oven perfect. They were incredibly light, and I think the might have floated into the dining room of their own accord.

—Bartow Culp

SHERI CASTLE'S SWEET POTATO BISCUIT BREAD PUDDING WITH BOURBON-PECAN CARMEL SAUCE

The point of bread pudding is to use leftover bread, whatever the daily bread might be. I've made biscuit bread pudding for years, but one day when I decided to use leftover sweet potato biscuits, a family favorite was born. Unlike pudding made from crusty yeast bread, the tender biscuits nearly dissolve in the sweet custard, so biscuit pudding is very soft. With the Bourbon-Pecan Caramel Sauce, it's wonderful. Really, really sweet, but heavenly.

—Sheri Castle

Makes 8 servings

3 large eggs
¾ cup sugar
1 tablespoon pure vanilla extract
2 cups half-and-half
4 cups loosely crumbled Sweet Potato Biscuits (6 to 8 biscuits) (see page 48)
¼ cup dried cherries or golden raisins

Preheat the oven to 350 degrees. Butter a 1½-quart baking dish. The pudding bakes in a water bath, so set the dish inside a larger baking dish.

Whisk the eggs in a large bowl until the yolks and whites are blended. Whisk in the sugar, vanilla and half-and-half. Stir in the biscuits and cherries. Pour into the prepared 1½-quart baking dish. Add enough very hot tap water to the outer dish to come halfway up the outside of the inner baking dish. Bake until the top is puffed and the pudding is just set, about 50 minutes. A thin knife inserted about 1 inch from the center should come out moist but not wet.

Remove the pudding from the oven and let it sit in the hot water bath for 5 minutes before serving warm with the Bourbon-Pecan Caramel Sauce.

BOURBON-PECAN CARAMEL SAUCE

This sauce is a liquid praline and is almost too good. There are people who will pretend they hear something in the backyard and offer to be an intrepid investigator when they are actually sneaking into the kitchen to eat this straight from the jar by the spoonful. Or so I am told.

—Sheri Castle

Makes about 2 cups

1¼ cups sugar
½ cup water
¼ cup light corn syrup
1¼ cups whipping cream
1 cup coarsely chopped pecans, toasted
2 tablespoons bourbon
½ teaspoon large-crystal garnishing salt, such as fleur de sel or Maldon, or kosher salt

Stir together the sugar, water and corn syrup in a large, heavy saucepan. Cook over medium heat without stirring until the sugar dissolves and turns the color of amber, about 7 minutes. Use a pastry brush dipped in cold water to wash down the sugar crystals on the side of the pan. Immediately remove from the heat and carefully pour in the cream; it will bubble vigorously and the caramel will harden. Stir over low heat until the mixture is smooth.

Bring the sauce to a boil and cook until it thickens enough to lightly coat the back of a spoon, stirring often, about 3 minutes. Remove from the heat and stir in the pecans, bourbon and salt. Serve warm or let cool. Then cover and refrigerate for up to 1 week. Reheat gently for serving.

Three of my grandparents were raised and lived in Conway, South Carolina. This is Horry County, black-water swamp and farmland, where three lines of my blood have farmed for three hundred years. They grew almost everything they ate, including hundreds of acres of corn. But I'm disappointed that cornmeal didn't appear on the table very much. I adore anything made from it [but] didn't end up with any family recipes. I think, if you have to feed cows and hogs, all the corn goes to them. I do know that my grandparents' 1929 wedding cake was cornbread, with chocolate icing. They had much more land than money, so maybe cornmeal was a special-occasion ingredient.

I've never tried to make my Conway grandma's biscuits. I spent thousands of hours with her and learned much. But I don't even think her four daughters have attempted the biscuits. What would be the point? They cannot be replicated, as we all learned with her pecan pie. Best to remember that she made them almost every meal, for unpredictable and large crowds, and that is a lifetime accomplishment. A big enameled tub stored the flour. Make a depression in the flour for the unmeasured grease and milk, mash it and gather just the right amount of flour until it's dough. I believe magic was involved. Grandma didn't roll and cut—not enough room on the counter. She formed balls, laid them on the black pan and flattened with four fingers. They formed gentle smooth domes. I haven't had one in twenty-eight years, and I can taste that biscuit right now.

How could there have always been leftover biscuits? Another mystery. But they went straight into the pie safe. Years after the cooking stopped, the safe still smelled like biscuits. A great thing about yesterday's biscuit: in Horry County, after the hogs have been fed, the wood cut, the fire built under the cast-iron tub for bathing [and] the cotton picked, nobody has time or money for a pie. Poke a hole in the biscuit with your finger, make a reservoir, pour in molasses. Depending on the size of your finger, individualized dessert. I'm very proud to have learned this from my grandma. There's a strong argument that pecan pie is not better than a molasses biscuit.

—Jimmy Holcomb

SWEET BREAKFAST MOLASSES BISCUIT "BUNS"

Serves 8

1 stick butter
¼ cup molasses
¼ cup light brown sugar
1 teaspoon cinnamon
1 recipe Marilyn's Biscuits, see page 24

Preheat oven to 425 degrees. Combine butter, molasses, sugar and cinnamon in a small saucepan over medium heat. Cook until sugar is melted, stirring often. Pour into a buttered 8-inch cake pan or skillet.

Prepare Marilyn's Biscuits according to recipe instructions and place in pan tightly together. Butter liberally as in biscuit instructions and bake 20 to 25 minutes. Remove from the oven when lightly browned, brush again with butter and turn out onto a cutting board. Serve warm.

DARRYL WILLIAMS'S WEST TEXAS COWBOY SOURDOUGH BISCUITS

For several years I attended an annual all-male overnight fishing trip held by some rancher friends on the banks of one of the branches of the Brazos River running through a parcel of one of the legendary West Texas cattle ranches. Menus included classic ranch fare—grilled steaks, beans, fish (if we caught enough), hamburgers, barbecue of all sorts and, of course, lots of beer. The highlight, though, was a chuck wagon breakfast. The cooks would rise before everyone else, stir up the fires that had been stoked for the night and begin to cook huge slabs of sliced bacon and scrambled eggs in army-surplus ammunition cans set over the open fires. They also stirred up the dough for sourdough biscuits to be baked in old-fashioned spiders (three-legged Dutch ovens with flat lids) that would be buried in the coals of the campfires. This was a feast for a king—or, at least, some satisfied West Texas cowmen.

—Darryl Williams

Makes about 10 to 15 biscuits

½ cup sourdough starter, recipe follows
1 cup milk
2½ cups all-purpose flour
¾ teaspoon salt
1 tablespoon sugar
1 teaspoon baking powder
½ teaspoon baking soda
bacon grease from bacon cooked earlier (or 2 tablespoons oil and 2 tablespoons melted butter)

The night before, dissolve the starter thoroughly in the milk. Be sure to use a large metal container that can be covered securely to keep out any varmints—and people—during the night.

Thoroughly stir in 1 cup flour, cover securely, and set in a warm place, not too close to the fire, but also not out in the cold night air.

In the morning, combine the remaining 1½ cups flour, salt, sugar, baking powder and baking soda and add to the starter mixture from the night before. Using clean hands, combine into a soft dough. Knead in the metal container for a few minutes and let rest.

In the meantime, prepare the fire: smother any active flames and with a hoe or shovel pull the coals to the edge of the fire pit so that your spider or Dutch oven will fit easily into the hole.

Here, on one of the SMS ranches near Spur, Texas, in 1939, the cook prepares to feed cowboys from the chuck wagon. With no regular oven to use, biscuits were made in a Dutch oven (seen behind the cook). Dough was cooked by placing the cast-iron pot on a bed of hot coals and piling more coals on the lid. *Photo by Russell Lee, Courtesy Library of Congress.*

This type of cast-iron Dutch oven, often called a spider, sits on three legs that make it more useful in a bed of hot coals than on a stovetop or in an oven. *Photo by Darryl Williams.*

On a flat, lightly floured surface, pat the dough into a round about a ½ inch thick. Then cut individual biscuits. If this is a high-class cookout, use a 2½-inch biscuit cutter. Otherwise, use your cleanest knife to cut 2-inch squares.

Dip each biscuit in bacon grease and place it in the bottom of the cast iron pot until the pot is completely full. Put the lid on the pot and lower the whole thing into the prepared cooking pit using the bale attached to the pot and a hook or hoe.

With the hoe or shovel, layer some of the coals on the top of the cast-iron pot—enough to evenly cover the lid.

Bake for about 30 to 35 minutes. It is very hard to check the baking, but you can try to remove the coals from the lid to check. Just remember to put them back on top if you bake some more.

If you are baking at home, dip each biscuit in melted bacon grease or a combination of oil and melted butter (bacon grease may be too strong a flavor for a home meal). Arrange the biscuits in a 10-inch cast-iron skillet. Bake in a preheated oven at 375 degrees for 30 to 35 minutes.

Serve immediately. Cold cowboy sourdough biscuits get as hard as a rock.

Sourdough Starter

Sourdough starter can last a long time if it is properly cared for. Starter can be easily kept out of the way in a closed jar in the back of the refrigerator for years, but if you haven't used it for several months, it will have to be revived before using it. If you can't revive it, don't worry. It is easy enough to start a new one. Sourdough is slower than commercial yeast, so breads made with it often do not rise as much. For that reason, breads made with sourdough alone require a long rise or fermentation, but starter can still be used for flavoring. The most successful recipes are for biscuits, cornbread, pancakes, traditional country loaves and French bread.

TRADITIONAL METHOD I

2 cups milk
2 cups all-purpose flour

Mix the milk and flour together in a large ceramic bowl until smooth. Set uncovered in a warm kitchen for 2 to 5 days, stirring occasionally. When the mixture is bubbly and has a yeasty, sour smell, the starter is ready.

Store well covered in a glass or ceramic container on the counter or in the middle of the refrigerator. Keep at least 3 cups on hand.

Replenish by stirring in equal portions of milk and flour

TRADITIONAL METHOD II

1 cup all-purpose flour
1 cup water

In a 4-cup or larger clear glass jar, mix the flour and water into a smooth paste. Set uncovered in a warm place. The kitchen is usually the best choice.

Every day, check the mixture for bubbles, remove any tough skin that has formed on the top, pour off about half the mixture and add an additional ½ cup flour and ½ cup water, stirring to form a smooth paste.

Repeat this process each day until the mixture is covered with bubbles and is doubled in size or so. You should observe frequently during the day and evening because a good starter will eventually collapse from its own weight and lose volume.

You will probably need to repeat the process for a week or more before you have established a good starter. After that, you should repeat the replenishment process for at least a couple of days before you plan to bake. You may store the starter in the refrigerator, but that is not necessary and even encourages less desirable things to grow and discolor the mix. If that happens, pour off the discolored top part, keeping just a few tablespoons of the starter to rejuvenate your stock.

NEW METHOD

2 cups all-purpose flour
2 cups water or milk
1 tablespoon sugar
½ package dry yeast

Mix the flour, milk and sugar together into a smooth batter. Sprinkle the yeast over the surface and stir in. Allow to stand uncovered in a warm kitchen until the mixture is bubbly and has a good aroma. The starter is ready.

Store and replenish as above.

If you have not used the starter for a long time, you may need to add milk and flour in equal amounts with a tablespoon of sugar and let the mixture stand overnight before using.

BLACKBERRY COBBLER

When I was young we used to pick wild blackberries in Georgia fields. They were a little smaller and more tart than the cultivated blackberries you often find today. Regardless of which blackberry type you use, this delicious Southern classic dessert counts as a bread because the crust is essentially biscuits.

—Marilyn Markel

Serves 6

For the Filling
6 cups blackberries
¼ to ½ cup sugar, depending on the tartness of the berries
2 teaspoons lemon zest
¼ cup Chambord
2 tablespoons cornstarch

For the Crust
1¼ cups self-rising flour
pinch baking soda
¼ teaspoon salt
2 tablespoons sugar
3 tablespoons butter, cubed, plus 4 tablespoons melted
⅔ cup buttermilk, or more

Preheat the oven to 400 degrees.

Combine blackberries, sugar, lemon zest, liqueur and cornstarch. Set aside.

Butter a 9-inch skillet or a 9 by 12 baking dish. Spoon the fruit mixture into the skillet.

In a medium mixing bowl, combine self-rising flour, baking soda, salt and sugar. Stir with a pastry blender. Cut in the cubed butter with a pastry blender until mixture resembles coarse meal.

Stir in the buttermilk with a spatula. Drop dough by spoonfuls onto fruit mixture.

Brush with the melted butter and place in the oven. Bake about 45 minutes, or until lightly browned. Brush liberally with butter.

While recording the bread memories of fellow Southerners for this book, I tried to recall my own. I grew up in Texas and my grandmother lived nearby. She was a good cook, but I don't ever remember her making bread of any type. I'm not saying she didn't; it just wasn't memorable to me (unlike her salmon croquettes or turkey curry, which was made with Thanksgiving leftovers). I do remember my mother sometimes made slightly sweet corn sticks in the cast-iron pans shaped like ears of corn. They were best right out of the oven when the butter melted on them, but I think I remember them now for the funny shape as much as I do for the taste. I also remember eating a lot of tortillas and often as part of a meal without any relation to traditional Mexican cuisine.

It wasn't until I went to college in Chapel Hill, North Carolina, that I made new bread memories. There, I discovered late-night biscuits at a place called Time Out on Franklin Street. After an evening of beer-soaked adventures about town, we would stumble into this establishment, which I don't think I ever visited during daylight hours. With what remaining change we could scrape together, we would order a biscuit and hope they had bones for sale. Bones, which came in a tinfoil packet, were the leftovers of fried chicken after the meat had been pulled off to make full price chicken biscuits. If they had any left (we weren't the only ones with this same idea), we would buy them for next to nothing and pick over the carcasses for any tasty bits to add to our biscuit. The memories are a bit hazy for reasons other than time, but I still sometimes crave those fluffy biscuits.

—Chris Holaday

HISTORY'S BISCUITS

MISSISSIPPI BISCUITS

Two cups of flour,
One-fourth teaspoonful of soda,
One and one-half teaspoonsful of baking powder,
One teaspoonful of salt,
Two tablespoonfuls of lard.

Mix flour, baking powder and salt. Then work in lightly the lard and mix with sufficient milk to make soft dough. Roll thin, cut into biscuits with small biscuit cutter and bake in quick oven.

—from *Aunt Caroline's Dixieland Recipes*, 1922

Georgia Sweet Potato Biscuit

One pint of flour, one pint of potato, one-half cupful of granulated sugar, one tablespoon butter, one teaspoonful of soda, and buttermilk to mix. The potatoes should be baked, instead of boiled, and run through a meat-chopper before measuring. Mix the dough and allow to stand several hours before making out the biscuit. Bake slowly in a moderate oven.

—from *Echoes of Southern Kitchens*, 1916

Tavern Biscuit

To one pound of flour, add half a pound of sugar, half a pound of butter, some mace and nutmeg powdered, and a glass of brandy or wine; wet it with milk, and when well kneaded, roll it thin, cut it in shapes, and bake quickly.

—from *The Virginia Housewife*, 1838

Virginia Beaten Biscuit

One quart of sifted flour, one teaspoon of salt, one-fourth pound of butter, milk to moisten. Put flour in a bowl, add the salt, then rub the butter into it with the hands, add the milk gradually until just moist. Work and knead until smooth and elastic, then put the dough on a block and beat until full of bubbles. Roll one-half inch thick, cut in small round cakes, stick with a fork, and bake in a quick oven, a light brown.

—from *Echoes of Southern Kitchens*, 1916

Biscuits have always been the food of every Southerner, rich or poor. Here a migrant farm worker makes biscuits in her tent home in Mercedes, Texas, during the Great Depression. *Photo by Russell Lee, courtesy Library of Congress.*

CHEESE BISCUITS

Put in a pan and brown in the oven.

Two cupsful of flour, two teaspoons full of baking powder, two heaping tablespoonsful lard, one-half cup of milk, one-fourth teaspoonful salt. Mix these ingredients as for biscuits. Roll thin and divide in two parts. Spread grated cheese on half of the dough, lay the other half of the dough over the cheese, cut out with cutter and bake.

—from *Echoes of Southern Kitchens,* 1916

Chapter 4
THANK THE MILLER

For wheat and corn to make it from the field to the bread, it has to be ground into a fine meal. As the first humans to do this quickly discovered, it was a very labor-intensive process. The dried corn or wheat had to be beaten with a rock and pounded over and over until it reached the right texture. One can only imagine how long it would take to produce enough meal to fill the bags we see in stores today.

When the Europeans came to the New World, they brought with them a more efficient way of milling—crushing grains between two huge round stones with notched surfaces. One stone would rotate against the other with slow revolutions to prevent heat buildup and help the meal retain its essential oils and flavor.

The power source for the grinding was a plentiful one: water. It took a bit of ingenuity and engineering—not to mention backbreaking labor—to harness the power of water, however. A narrow canal, or race, was dug, and water was diverted into it and directed toward a large wheel attached to the mill building. The force of the water turned the wheel, and that power was transferred—usually through gears and leather belts—to the turning stone. Speed was controlled by the amount of water let into the race through sluice gates. To maintain a constant water supply, dams were often built across creeks.

Long before locally sourced foods became all the rage, gristmills were helping area farmers reach nearby consumers. The farmers brought their corn and wheat to the miller, who ground and bagged it. Farmers kept some of what was produced for their own needs and bartered with or sold the rest. For their fee, millers often kept a percentage of the meal to sell themselves under their own name. The products of these mills developed loyal followings, and many old cooks were devoted fans of one brand or another. The texture, the flavor—they swore they could taste a difference.

Most of these local water-powered mills are gone today, but a few still exist. Some are preserved as historic sites, such as Virginia's picturesque Mabry Mill. Located on the Blue Ridge Parkway, it has been visited by countless tourist over

Aderholdt Mill, seen here in a 1935 photo, is situated on the Tallaseehatchee Creek in Calhoun County, Alabama. It began operation in 1836 and closed in the 1970s. *Courtesy Library of Congress.*

Waterwheel at Logan Maxwell's gristmill, three miles from Cornelia, Georgia, in 1936. *Photo by Carl Mydans, courtesy Library of Congress.*

Opposite, bottom: Bringing home meal from the cooperative gristmill, Gee's Bend, Alabama, in 1939. *Photo by Marion Post Wolcott, courtesy Library of Congress.*

the years. A few others, like the Old Mill of Guilford in North Carolina, are still in operation. That mill was grinding corn at the time of the American Revolution in a manner not much different from that of today. Sciple's Water Mill in DeKalb, Mississippi, isn't much younger and was even featured on the television show *Dirty Jobs* in 2010.

Small water mills sometimes evolved into larger businesses that still served a local or regional area. Some converted to roller mills, which used large metal rollers instead of stones and were powered by electricity or fossil fuels. Today, much of the nation's demand for cornmeal and flour is met by large commercial mills, many of which ship nationwide. You can also sometimes get freshly ground mill at farmers' markets.

Though most of the small mills that once dotted the South have vanished, signs remain of how prevalent and important to local economies they once were. Take a

When Spanish missionaries arrived in what is now Texas and Louisiana, they brought milling technology with them. This simple mill was built at Mission San José in San Antonio, Texas, in 1794. Water was directed into the basement to turn this wheel, which was connected by shaft to a millstone directly above. Though native corn grew easily in the area, the missionaries preferred familiar wheat and tried to encourage the local Indian population to accept it. *Courtesy Library of Congress.*

Womack's Mill was constructed in 1909 in Caswell County, North Carolina, on the site of an earlier mill. In operation until 1955, it used one set of stones and four wheat roller mills (seen here around 1970). *Photo by Jet Lowe, courtesy Library of Congress.*

Flour and meal produced by millers from across the South. *Authors' collection.*

walk down almost any creek or small river in the region, and it is not uncommon to come across the remains of dams and overgrown raceways. Show your respect if you do—Southern bread would never have reached the cultural status it has without these industrious mills.

Chapter 5
CORNBREAD

Famed *New York Times* food critic and Mississippi native Craig Claiborne once said, "There are more recipes for cornbread than there are magnolia trees in the South."

That may be a slight exaggeration, but the reason for so many cornbread recipes is simple: it is delicious and can be served with so many things. Whether cooked in the oven in a black, well-loved cast-iron skillet or fried on the stovetop, cornmeal can be turned into many types of bread. No one agrees on which is best, and converting someone from the method taught by their grandmother is impossible.

The one thing many Southerners probably do agree on concerning cornbread is that there is no addition of sugar. In 1920, Colonel George Bailey, a columnist and later editor of the *Houston Post*, published in his paper what he entitled "The Crime of Cornbread." In it, Bailey, who was a native of North Carolina, wrote, "Sugar in cornbread is an abomination. It ought to be made a crime. It violates every tradition of the South. It insults the palate. It mocks the art of cookery." He went on to say, "It was an idea born of the devil, planted in New England and sent to South by our enemies." The piece also claimed sugar in cornbread was "the mother of bolshevism and the germ of anarchy"; it "makes men trifling and women frivolous," and "it creates an appetite for moonshine." Humorous as it may have been, Bailey's rant showed how important it is to Southerners that sugar not invade cornbread.

Nearly the iconic equal of the biscuit is the hushpuppy. Whether deep-fried, crunchy and round with a soft center or finger-shaped and dipped in butter, these small treats have a cloudy history steeped in Southern folklore. Maybe, like the name implies, they were created to quiet whining dogs—or maybe not. Regardless, they have been a requirement at fish fries and barbecue restaurants across the South since before World War II.

Like with almost all Southern breads, there is dispute on how best to serve hushpuppies. Some like them with butter (or honey butter) while others swear they are best just plain and hot. Some recipes add onions; others don't. And some

Cornbread became very important during the Great Depression because meal was cheap. Here it is being made with relief meal, given out by the government, at a Civilian Conservation Corps camp in Virginia's Shenandoah National Park in 1935. *Photo by Arthur Rothstein, courtesy Library of Congress.*

hushpuppies are sweeter than others due to the amount of sugar added. The one thing all Southerners will agree on, however, is if you're serving fried catfish or pork barbecue, the meal isn't complete without a big batch of steaming hot hushpuppies.

MARILYN'S CORNBREAD

My grandfather used to love to eat cornbread with a bowl of buttermilk. I have not acquired that taste, but he enjoyed it so much. We liked the crispy edge so he would often cut off an edge for us instead of slicing. I don't think that made Grannie very happy, but she would never be angry with us.

—Marilyn Markel

Serves 8

¼ cup butter or bacon drippings
1½ cups coarse yellow cornmeal
½ cup flour
1 teaspoon salt
2 teaspoons baking powder
½ teaspoon baking soda
1 large egg
1½ cups buttermilk
serve with chow chow and pinto beans, recipes follow

Preheat oven to 450 degrees.

Heat fat in 9-inch skillet until sizzling.

Whisk the cornmeal, flour, salt, baking powder and baking soda in a large bowl. In a small bowl, whisk together the egg and buttermilk, pour it into the cornmeal mixture and stir with a spatula just until blended.

Pour the batter into the skillet. Put the skillet in the oven and bake until the cornbread tests clean, about 25 minutes. Turn out onto a cutting board or serving platter. Serve hot with plenty of butter or pimento cheese.

———•+•+•———

GREEN TOMATO CHOW CHOW

Chow chow in my family was always made to preserve the last of the garden before the first frost. We made green tomato chow chow at the end of the summer. Grannie and Granddaddy made their own batches and had a contest to decide whose was better. His was always hotter than hers, so feel free to add more hot peppers if you like. Any kind of peppers will do. Throughout the winter, we ate chow chow with pinto beans and a big slice of buttered cornbread—a little late summer garden in a jar to enjoy throughout the year.

—Marilyn Markel

½ cup pickling salt
10 cups peeled and chopped green tomatoes
2 red bell peppers, seeded and chopped
2 jalapeño peppers, seeded and chopped
1 onion, chopped
4 cucumbers, peeled and chopped
3 tablespoons pickling spice
1 cup sugar
3 cups cider vinegar
1 tablespoon mustard seed, lightly ground
1 teaspoon celery seed
1 teaspoon turmeric
1 teaspoon red pepper flakes

Salt the vegetables and let sit for 6 hours, or overnight. Strain and discard the liquid.

Put pickling spice in cheesecloth and secure with a string.

Bring sugar, vinegar, mustard seed, celery seed, turmeric, red pepper flakes and spice bag to a boil in a large nonreactive pot. Add drained vegetables and return to a boil.

Put into jars, wipe edges, seal and process in a hot canning bath or store in the refrigerator.

———•+•+•———

PINTO BEANS

We ate pinto beans all the time. A bowl with a piece of buttered cornbread and dollop of chow chow was a mainstay. The salt pork makes a flavorful potlikker and was our favorite, but you can certainly make a vegetarian version. Be sure to taste your beans for doneness.

—Marilyn Markel

Serves 8

1 pound dried pinto beans
4 ounces salt pork, sliced
1 onion, chopped
8 cups vegetable stock
salt and pepper, to taste

Examine beans and remove any stones or bad pieces.

Rinse beans thoroughly and cover with water by at least 4 inches. Soak overnight. Drain beans and rinse thoroughly. Wash pot and dry.

Add salt pork to pot and heat until sizzling. Add onion and sauté until soft. Return beans to the pot and cover with stock.

Simmer until tender, about 3 hours. Taste and season with salt and pepper.

To Cook in Pressure Cooker

Place soaked beans, fresh water and ham hock in the pressure cooker.

Set pressure to high and time for 30 minutes.

When pressure releases open cooker.

Salt and pepper beans to taste. Serve with chow chow.

The best fried cornbread ever was made by my grandmother Addie Mae Lester Williams Pettiford. We—her children, grandchildren and eventually great-grandchildren—all call her Mama. Three generations lived in our old wood-frame house that sat on a hill at the end of a dirt road in Roxboro, Person County, North Carolina. There we always had good food prepared by expert hands.

Mama cooked her cornbread in a heavy metal pan, and it was delicious. She mixed the batter from memory and, without a thermometer, always heated the oil to just the *right temperature to get a beautiful sizzle when the batter hit the pan. There it would rise and start to fill the air with a delicious toasted smell. To this day, I am not certain how she flipped cornbread that was at least eight inches in diameter to the opposite side so it would brown. I know it involved a pot top and a tremendous amount of dexterity.*

The cornbread was crusty on the outside and firm but moist on the inside. Mama sliced it into triangle shaped pieces for serving, then we slathered on butter that she made with milk from the cows she cared for daily. It was definitely what you'd call good eatin'.

—Tori Reid

CORNBREAD CROUTONS

Simple and easy, cornbread can be turned into a delicious crouton for salads. A ¼ cup minced country ham can also be tossed with cubes in the last five minutes of baking for an amazing flavor.

—Marilyn Markel

Marilyn's Cornbread leftovers, cut into cubes
olive oil, just enough to coat cubes
salt and pepper, to taste

Preheat oven to 375 degrees.

Place bread cubes on parchment-lined sheet pans. Toss with olive oil. Season with salt and pepper. Bake for 15 to 20 minutes, tossing occasionally until dried and crisp.

Serve on salads or soups.

CORNBREAD CAKES

Individual cornbread cakes can vary by size, so just scoop them out in whatever size you choose!

—Marilyn Markel

Serves 4–6

¾ cup coarse cornmeal

¼ cup flour

½ teaspoon salt

1 teaspoon baking powder

¼ teaspoon baking soda

1 egg yolk

¾ cup buttermilk

4 tablespoons bacon drippings

Whisk together the dry ingredients in a bowl. Add the egg yolk and buttermilk and stir with a spatula until blended.

Place the drippings in a cast-iron skillet. Heat over medium high until lightly smoking. Ladle in the batter by heaping tablespoons and cook until browned on the first side. Turn them over and flatten slightly as they finish cooking. Serve with Corn and Pea Succotash (recipe follows).

CORN AND PEA SUCCOTASH

Serves 4

2 cups fresh creamer peas, or any summer peas

2 tablespoons butter

2 tablespoons bacon fat

1 red bell pepper, diced

1 jalapeño, diced

3 garlic cloves

1 cup chicken or vegetable broth

1 teaspoon Worcestershire sauce

½ teaspoon minced thyme

dash hot sauce (optional)

4 ears corn, husked and cut off the cob

green onions, sliced on the diagonal
1 tablespoon chopped basil
4 medium leaves mint, julienned
chopped cooked bacon, for garnish (optional)

Rinse peas several times and drain in a colander. In a medium saucepan, cover peas with water by 3 inches and cook, simmering gently until tender, about 45 minutes. Remove any foam that forms on the top. Strain peas in a colander.

In skillet, melt butter and bacon fat and heat over medium high. Add the red pepper and jalapeño and sauté for a few minutes. Add the garlic and sauté until fragrant, just a couple minutes. Add the broth, Worcestershire, thyme, hot sauce (if using), corn and peas and reduce liquid almost all has evaporated. Serve garnished with green onions, basil, mint and bacon.

RICKY MOORE'S HUSH-HONEYS

Hushpuppies were a main staple in the household when I was growing up, we always had them with fried fish and barbecue. And we had lots of good cooks in the family. My recipe came about from a love of the Italian sweet fritter *zeppole*, which is essentially a fried dough with powdered sugar. I started thinking about it: zeppoles and hushpuppies, made sense to me. Both of them are a fried dough. I use polenta sometimes, and the texture changes the whole thing. That's how they came to be.

—Ricky Moore

2 cups yellow fine polenta (or fine cornmeal)
1 cup Italian Tipo 00 flour, such as Caputo
2 tablespoons sugar
1 tablespoon kosher salt
4 teaspoons baking powder
1 cup sour cream
¼ teaspoon hot sauce, such as Texas Pete
1 medium yellow onion, grated
¼ cup creamed corn
canola oil, for frying

Right: Chef Ricky Moore in the kitchen of his famed Durham, North Carolina eatery, Saltbox Seafood Joint.

Below: A perfect accompaniment: hush-honeys about to be served with fried black drum, coleslaw and fried potatoes.

SPICE SEASONING
1 tablespoon fennel seed toasted and ground
1 tablespoon coriander seed toasted and ground
1 tablespoon lemon peel dried and ground
2 teaspoons sea salt

In a large bowl, whisk together polenta, flour, sugar, salt and baking powder. In a medium bowl, whisk together sour cream, hot sauce, grated onion and creamed corn. Add cream mixture to dry ingredients and stir together with a spoon; let sit for 10 minutes.

Pour oil to a depth of 2 inches in a 6-quart Dutch oven and heat over medium high until a deep-fry thermometer reads 375 degrees. Transfer batter to a piping bag fitted with a ¾-inch-diameter round tip. Working in batches, pipe and cut 3-inch-long logs of batter into oil; fry until golden brown, 1 to 2 minutes. Transfer to paper towels to drain. Once drained, place in stainless bowl and toss with the spice seasoning. Serve on a warm plate and drizzle with honey.

DARRYL WILLIAMS'S HUSHPUPPIES

A fish fry is one of the great traditions of the entire South, but nowhere is it more on display than in east Texas and nearby Louisiana and Arkansas. The corners of these three states are so akin to one another that residents of the region call it the ArkLaTex. If you use that name, everyone knows where you live, and everyone knows what you think is important in life. Years ago, we lived in Shreveport, where one of the favorite eating haunts was the Cypress Inn. This huge, ramshackle place sat on the banks of the Cypress Bayou, and though it had a lot of choices on the menu, nobody ever went there except to eat the fried catfish dinner complete with hushpuppies.

The hushpuppies were golden balls of melt-in-your-mouth goodness—crispy outside, creamy inside with cornbread and chopped onions. Now, you may have had the eraser-shaped hush puppies in one of the big "country-style" chain restaurants, but those are a pale, tasteless copy of the real thing. The Cypress Inn had the real thing, and you could make a whole meal of hushpuppies alone. The catfish, of course, was equally delicious, with a golden, crunchy cornmeal crust and the flavorful, tender catfish inside.

—Darryl Williams

Makes about 30 hushpuppies

1½ cups yellow cornmeal
½ cup flour

1 teaspoon baking powder
½ teaspoon baking soda
1 teaspoon salt
¼ cup scallions, green tops only, chopped very finely
1 cup buttermilk
1 large egg
vegetable oil, for frying

Stir together the cornmeal, flour, baking powder, baking soda and salt so that they are completely mixed.

Add the chopped scallions, buttermilk and egg. Mix so that they are thoroughly combined.

By spoonful, drop the mixture into a deep pan with about 2 inches of vegetable oil that has been heated to 350 degrees, turning until the hushpuppies are golden brown on all sides.

Drain on paper towels and serve while still hot.

HUSHPUPPIES WITH COCKTAIL SAUCE

Makes about 20 hushpuppies and 1 cup of sauce

For Hushpuppies
2 tablespoons bacon grease, oil or butter, plus 2 cups oil for frying
2 cups loosely packed thinly sliced onions
1 cup yellow cornmeal
½ cup flour
2 teaspoons baking powder
½ teaspoon salt
1 egg
¾ cup buttermilk

Heat grease, butter or oil in a medium skillet. Add onion and cook on low heat until nicely browned and caramelized. This will take about 45 minutes to 1 hour, stirring occasionally.

Preheat oven to 200 degrees.

Mix dry ingredients well. Lightly beat egg and buttermilk and add cooled caramelized onions. Stir the buttermilk mixture into the dry ingredients. Mixture will be lumpy.

In a sturdy 2-quart saucepan, preheat oil to 350 degrees over medium high heat. If the handle of a wooden spoon is placed in the oil it will bubble vigorously at 350 degrees.

Using two spoons, drop dough in spoonfuls into hot oil and fry until they float. Turn them over to ensure even cooking, about 3 to 4 minutes per side. Remove from oil with a slotted spoon or fish spatula. Drain on paper towel–lined sheet pan and hold in the oven until ready to serve.

Note: The oil from this recipe can be reused. Cool to room temperature, strain and refrigerate.

For Cocktail Sauce
½ cup ketchup
¼ cup chili sauce
2 tablespoons lemon juice
1 tablespoon prepared horseradish (this will be spicy)
dash Worcestershire sauce

To make the cocktail sauce, combine the ketchup, chili sauce, lemon juice, horseradish and Worcestershire. Serve as a dipping sauce for the hushpuppies.

I don't know my mother's hushpuppy recipe, but [I know] it was onionless and she dropped them into the hot grease with a butter knife. The grease pot was kept in the refrigerator and reused for an indeterminate amount of time. The knife-shaped hushpuppies were designed, probably, for maximum fried surface area. Oh, very good. We did go to many barbecue and Calabash-style seafood places. The dirty little secret about North Carolina is that the barbecue is all pretty indistinguishable. But there is no excuse for an inferior hushpuppy. I think we settled on the places with perfect hushpuppies.

—*Jimmy Holcomb*

TEX-MEX CORNBREAD

Perhaps originating in Texas, this spicy cornbread makes a perfect partner for a bowl of chili and a cold beer. If you're not a big fan of heat in your cornbread, just cut the chili powder and jalapeños in half. You'll still get the great taste.

—Marilyn Markel

Serves 8

1½ cups coarse yellow cornmeal (stone ground)

½ cup flour

1 teaspoon salt

2 teaspoons baking powder

½ teaspoon baking soda

1 teaspoon ground cumin

1 teaspoon chili powder

1 cup corn, about 2 ears cut from the cob

½ cup chopped green onion, white and green parts

¼ cup diced pickled jalapeño

1 cup grated cheddar cheese

1 large egg

1½ cups buttermilk

¼ cup butter or bacon drippings

Preheat oven to 450 degrees.

Whisk the dry ingredients in a large bowl. Stir in the corn, green onion, jalapeño and cheese.

In a small bowl, or measuring cup, whisk together the egg and buttermilk. Pour into the cornmeal mixture and stir until just blended.

Put fat in a 9-inch skillet and melt in the oven until hot.

Remove the skillet from the oven and pour in the batter. Bake until brown and crispy and a tester comes out clean, about 25 minutes.

SOUTHERN CORNBREAD PANZANELLA

Based on a traditional Tuscan dish, this is a terrific salad for New Year's Day. It has all of the famous traditional ingredients a good Southerner should eat to start the New Year off properly.

—Marilyn Markel

Serves 6

1 pint fresh black-eyed peas, rinsed and drained
1 small bag frozen corn
½ batch Marilyn's Cornbread (page 70), cut into ½-inch cubes
6 green onions, rinsed and chopped
2 cups julienned baby collard greens or spinach
1 jalapeño pepper, seeded and chopped
1 large red bell pepper, finely chopped
1 pint cherry tomatoes, halved
2 cups grated sharp cheddar cheese
ranch dressing, recipe follows
chopped fresh parsley leaves, for garnish
¼ cup minced country ham

Cover black-eyed peas with water in a saucepan and cook until tender.

Drain and add the corn for a minute until cooked through. Allow to cool.

In the bottom of a large glass bowl, place cornbread cubes. Combine the peas, corn, onion, baby collards (or spinach), jalapeño, red bell pepper, tomatoes and cheese and layer on top of cornbread. Toss lightly. Serve with ranch dressing on the side. Garnish with fresh parsley and country ham, if desired.

RANCH DRESSING

Makes 1 cup

½ cup buttermilk
½ cup mayonnaise
½ teaspoon granulated garlic
1 teaspoon onion flakes
1 tablespoon minced chives
salt and pepper, to taste

Whisk together ingredients. Taste for seasoning.

BRINKLEY'S WHOLE WHEAT AND CORNMEAL PANCAKES

I often taught classes in North Carolina with local farmers. It was always a pleasure to teach with William and Dianne Brinkley. Brinkley Farms, in Creedmoor, North Carolina, is a fourth-generation farm where farming is a way of life. They have amazing products, including their own fresh-milled cornmeal, a family breakfast favorite. It is especially delicious with their freshly cured bacon from the farm.

—Marilyn Markel

Serves 4–6

1½ cups whole wheat flour
½ cup cornmeal
2 teaspoons baking powder
½ teaspoon baking soda
2 cups buttermilk
2 eggs
2 tablespoons honey
2 tablespoons oil
crisp bacon, for serving
pecan praline syrup, for serving

In a medium bowl combine the dry ingredients. Whisk together buttermilk, eggs, honey and stir into the dry mix using a spatula.

Heat oil in a skillet until shimmering. Ladle ¼ cup scoops of batter and cook until nicely browned on both sides. Keep warm in the oven until all batter is used. Top with crisp bacon and pecan praline syrup, if desired.

When I was in second grade at Florida State University Demonstration School in the mid-'50s, my dad—back from officer duty in Korea—was getting his PhD, and my mom was a Southern belle from Geneva County, Alabama, who worked hard to keep two small boys under control. We had a small house in Mabry Heights, the married-student housing neighborhood up the hill from the "Dem" School. On weekends in the school year, the dads would promote Wiffle Ball Golf Tournaments in the big, open rolling meadow in the middle of the neighborhood, and the wives and guests would sit and drink and gossip while the kids played all over. Then we'd make dinner for all.

Our dinner was always the big event, for up to a dozen or more families, friends and guests, since earlier in the day some of the guys had made a fresh-fish run down to the coast to get the best in red snapper, Apalachicola oysters and Gulf shrimp. My mom and others in the know would make the fixins. She was our hushpuppy queen and would do big batches and roll up dozens of them for all the gang, many of them from other countries and places across America. Many got their first taste of hushpuppies at FSU. We kids were luckier. We were at all the parties. Sweet, hand-rolled hushpuppies—with lots of chopped onion, fresh from the kitchen and ready for a rolling boil in big old iron pots—were the best, along with a table-size feast of fried seafood and coleslaw and all the potluck stuff. After the sun went down, we'd chase fireflies, and they'd keep the big boiling pots going ("Kids, stay away from the cooking!") into the early evening.

—Dennis Hermanson

OYSTER, COUNTRY HAM AND PORCINI STUFFING

Makes 8 servings

7 cups 1-inch-cubed crusty white bread

7 cups 1-inch-cubed cornbread

1 pound shucked oysters, or you can use 6 to 8 ounces canned oysters

1 stick butter

4 ounces country ham, minced

2 cups diced celery

3 cups diced onion

½ cup dried porcinis, rehydrated in boiling water, drained and finely chopped

½ teaspoon salt

½ teaspoon pepper

2 tablespoons chopped fresh sage leaves

1 tablespoon fresh minced thyme

½ cup chopped fresh flat-leaf parsley

3 eggs

4 cups chicken or turkey stock

Toast the breadcrumbs and cornbread on a sheet pan at 375 degrees for about 20 minutes, until golden.

Drain and rinse the oysters in a colander.

In a skillet, heat the butter over medium until melted. Add the country ham, celery, onion and mushrooms. Sprinkle with salt and pepper. Cook until softened, stirring often, about 15 minutes. Stir in the oysters, sage, thyme and parsley.

Combine the bread cubes and the cooled cooked vegetables in a large bowl.

Whisk the eggs in a small bowl. Combine the eggs and the stock. Add eggs and stock to the stuffing and stir well. Place in a buttered casserole dish and bake, covered, for 30 minutes. Then uncover and bake until golden brown, about 20 more minutes.

I kind of picked up my mother's cornbread recipe. I like the texture of cornbread because it's got the grain to it, and it doesn't get soft in the middle and chewy. I make it a lot, usually twice a week, maybe more. It's a very simple recipe. I do it a little bit differently. It's not crumbly because I add flour. I don't measure, I just do it by the eye. I guess I was taught doing it by the eye instead of [with] the measuring cup. I just pour it in the bowl. If I wanted to measure it, I'd say it's around two cups of meal and one of flour, depends on the size pan, but 2 to 1. Then I add the milk and mix it until it gets not as thin a consistency as pancake batter but not as thick as biscuits. I get my skillet hot before I pour my batter in because it gives it the crunch when you bake it. I put it in the oven at 400 degrees, and when the top starts turning medium brown you take it out. I'm a country girl, so soup beans, green beans, fried taters—if you've got those on your meal list, you have to have cornbread. And it's good with just milk. That was one of my dad's favorites,

Glenda Flanary's cornbread. *Photo by Wes Flanary.*

cornbread and milk. A glass of sweet milk, crumble your cornbread up in there and just go to town; it's like a dessert. Even buttermilk. I love it in buttermilk, too. You just have to try it.

—Glenda Flanary

SAUSAGE STUFFING MUFFINS

Makes 12 muffins

3 cups 1-inch-cubed cornbread
½ pound sausage
½ stick butter
½ cup diced celery
¾ cup diced onion

salt and pepper, to taste

1 teaspoon fresh minced thyme, removed from woody stems

2 tablespoons chopped fresh flat-leaf parsley

1 egg

1 cup chicken or turkey stock, or more if needed

Toast the cornbread on a sheet pan at 375 degrees for about 20 minutes, until golden.

Cook sausage, breaking into small pieces, in a skillet over medium heat until crispy. Transfer to paper towel–lined tray or plate. Pour off excess fat, retaining about 2 tablespoons in the skillet.

Add the celery and onion to the skillet and cook over medium heat, stirring often, about 15 minutes. Season lightly with salt and pepper. Stir in thyme and parsley.

Combine the bread cubes and the cooked and cooled vegetables in a large bowl.

Beat the eggs in a small bowl. Add eggs and stock to the stuffing mixture and stir well. Place in buttered baking muffin tins and bake for 30 minutes.

JENNIE BUNCH'S SPOON BREAD WITH LEMON CREAM AND SHRIMP

Jennie Bunch was one of my grandmother's best friends from Currituck County, North Carolina. She put this recipe in a local church cookbook, and it was the cornbread I grew up with. It is sweet and eggy and not dry. To me this is what cornbread should taste like.

—Willard Doxey

Serves 6

1½ cups yellow cornmeal

½ cup sugar

1 teaspoon salt

2 cups water

2 cups milk

4 eggs

1 stick butter

1 batch Lemon Cream, recipe follows

1 pound shrimp, cleaned and cooked

Preheat oven to in 400 degrees.

Mix cornmeal, sugar, salt and water in a medium saucepan. Cook over medium heat until thick. Remove from heat and add the milk and eggs. Blend well. Put the butter in a 9 by 9 baking dish and place in the preheated oven. Remove the pan from the oven once the butter is melted and pour mixture into the pan spreading out in the butter.

Bake for about 45 minutes. Cool slightly and cut into serving-size pieces or spoon out.

LEMON CREAM

4 tablespoons butter
1 cup heavy cream
1 tablespoon fresh lemon juice
zest of 2 lemons

Bring the butter and cream to a boil over medium high heat. Add the lemon juice and stir.

Stir in the zest and continue to cook on medium-low heat, stirring occasionally until the sauce is thick and reduced.

Plating: Cut the spoon bread into squares and then triangles. Place three triangles on the plate, top with cooked shrimp and lemon cream.

My grandmother Carrie Baldwin Gilbert made her cornbread in a big cast-iron skillet with half an inch of oil in the bottom. She heated it up and dropped in the batter, which was made with a light-yellow stone-ground meal that wasn't too fine. However big you made the drop is what you got. The cornbread came out browned on the bottom but still soft on the top. They were sort of similar to the cornsticks you get in some barbecue restaurants, but those are submerged in oil so [they're] crispy all around. I've tried to make them but I can't seem to get the consistency of the cornmeal right. I asked my mother and she said it was a specific type of meal. I need to find it.

—Craig Gilbert

———•••———

TAMALES

Tamales are very popular in Texas for Christmas Eve. Make the filling a day or two before assembling the tamales. The filling, as well as the tamales, freeze well. Freeze the tamales after assembly, before cooking.

—Marilyn Markel

Makes about 25–30 tamales

30 dried cornhusks
1½ quarts boiling water, plus a ¼ cup
2 cups masa harina
2 cups warm chicken stock
1 teaspoon salt
1 cup diced lard
1 teaspoon baking powder
Pork Filling for Tamales, recipe follows

Place cornhusks in a large bowl and submerge with a weight. Add boiling water to cover and let soak while preparing remaining ingredients.

Place masa harina in the bowl of an electric mixer. Beating at low speed, add the chicken stock. Then increase speed to medium and beat well for 5 minutes.

Gradually add salt and lard cubes and continue beating for 10 minutes. The dough should be light and fluffy.

Dissolve baking powder in ¼ cup water and add to dough. Beat 5 more minutes until very light and fluffy.

Drain cornhusks. Lay out a clean kitchen towel. Remove 1 cornhusk and lightly dry on the towel on both sides. Spread 2 to 3 tablespoons (cornhusks vary in size) of masa mixture over the cornhusk and spread all the way to both edges on the wide top side, but about 2 inches from the smaller triangle side.

Top masa dough with approximately 1½ tablespoons pork filling, starting a ½ inch in from the edge closest to you and spreading it down the 3-inch length of the dough.

Roll the tamale to enclose the filling, ending with a cigar shaped cylinder that is filled almost to the cut end and empty and pointed on the other.

Fold the empty triangle edge and tie with a torn-off piece of husk. It's best to use misshapen husks and tear off a ½ inch at a time.

Bring water in a large tamale pot, or pot with an insert basket, to a boil. Be sure the water is not touching the basket.

Place all tamales upright (open side facing up) in the steamer basket and cook over the simmering water about an hour. Keep checking to ensure the water in the bottom of the pot does not dry out.

Serve with salsa of your choice.

PORK FILLING FOR TAMALES

Makes enough for 2–3 dozen tamales

6 dried ancho chiles

4 cups water

1 large onion, peeled and cut in chunks

4 cloves garlic, peeled

1 teaspoon Mexican oregano, crumbled

2 tablespoons ground cumin

1 orange, zested

3½ to 4 pounds pork butt, trimmed and cut in four pieces

3 teaspoons salt

2 teaspoons pepper

3 tablespoons grapeseed or other neutral oil

2 tablespoons hot sauce (optional)

Toast anchos in a dry skillet over high heat until fragrant. Add water and bring it to a boil. Soak for 1 to 3 hours.

Preheat oven to 300 degrees.

Remove chiles from soaking liquid, reserving liquid. Remove stems and seeds from the chiles and place them in a blender with onions, garlic and 2 cups of the soaking liquid. Cover and puree until smooth.

Add the oregano, cumin and orange zest to the puree in the blender.

Heat a medium to large Dutch oven over medium high. Season the meat on all sides with salt and pepper. Add the oil and heat until shimmering. Sear the pork on all sides until deeply golden brown.

Add the puree and bring to a simmer. Cover and place in the oven to cook for 5 hours, or until pork falls apart.

Refrigerate overnight.

The following day remove any solidified pieces of pork fat in the juice. Shred the meat with two forks.

CORNBREAD HERITAGE

MISSISSIPPI CORN BREAD

One quart of buttermilk, two eggs, three spoonfuls of butter, and a teaspoon of saleratus; stir in meal, to the milk, until it is as thick as buckwheat batter. Bake in squares about one inch thick. It will require half an hour in a hot oven. If it is not nice, it will be because you have put in too much meal, and made the batter too thick. But try again, and you will succeed.

—from *La Cuisine Creole*, 1885

VIRGINIA ASH CAKE

Add a teaspoonful of salt to a quart of sifted corn meal. Make up with water and knead well. Make into round, flat cakes. Sweep a clean place on the hottest part of the hearth. Put the cake on it and cover it with hot wood ashes. Wash and wipe it dry, before eating it. Sometimes a cabbage leaf is placed under it, and one over it, before baking, in which case it need not be washed.

—from *Housekeeping in Old Virginia*, 1878

SPOON BREAD

One and a half cups of meal, one and a half cups of milk, three eggs, a tablespoonful of lard, a tablespoonful of butter, two tea-spoonfuls of baking powder. Scald the meal thoroughly with hot water, then stir in the eggs, melted butter and lard, then the milk, and lastly the baking powder. Be careful to have a thin batter.

—from *Southern Recipes, Tested by Myself*, 1913

OWENDAW CORN BREAD

Take about two tea-cups of hommony [*sic*], and while hot mix with it a very large spoonful of butter (good lard will do); beat four eggs very light, and stir them into the hommony; next add about a pint of milk, gradually stirred in; and lastly, half pint of corn meal. The batter should be of the consistency of a rich boiled custard; if thicker, add a little more milk. Bake with a good deal of heat at the bottom of the oven, and not too much at the top, so as to allow it to rise. The pan in which it is baked ought to be a deep one, to allow space for rising. It has the appearance, when cooked, of a baked batter pudding, and when rich, and well mixed, it has almost the delicacy of a baked custard.

—from *The Carolina Housewife*, 1847

CRACKLIN BREAD

Take one quart sifted corn meal and a teacup of cracklins. Rub the latter in the meal as fine as you can. Add a teaspoonful of salt and make up with warm water into a stiff dough. Make into pones, and eat hot.

—from *Housekeeping in Old Virginia*, 1878

BACHELOR'S PONE

Melt a piece of butter the size of an egg in some new milk. Beat the yolks of five or six eggs very light, stir into the milk some Indian meal, then add the eggs, and a little salt, make it rather stiffer than a flour pudding; bake it in a quick oven, in a buttered pan, or in small pattypans. When you serve it, break it, as the knife spoils it.

—from *The Carolina Housewife*, 1847

COUCHE COUCHE

Make a paste as you make for corn bread. Sweeten it with sugar. Instead of putting it in a pan, you grease a pot with lard, and as the paste cooks to the side of the pot, you scrape it off with a spoon. Do that five or six times, until all your paste is cooked. It is delicious for breakfast with coffee. The Southern children are very fond of it with milk.

—from *Cooking in Old Creole Days*, 1903

Hominy Bread

Mix with two teacups of hot hominy a very large spoonful of butter. Beat two eggs very light and stir into the hominy. Next add a pint of milk, gradually stirring it in. Lastly, add half a pint of corn meal. The batter should be of the consistency of rich boiled custard. If thicker, add a little more milk. Bake with a good deal of heat at the bottom, but not so much at the top. Bake in a deep pan, allowing space for rising. When done, it looks like a baked batter pudding.

—from *Housekeeping in Old Virginia*, 1878

The modern bread baker's arsenal (clockwise from top left): melon baller (for Marilyn's Biscuits recipe), cooling rack, rolling pin, dough scraper (for cleaning off counters), several sizes of large bowls, pastry blender (for cutting in shortening), biscuit cutters (nice and sharp) and a set of measuring spoons and cups.

Chapter 6
OTHER BREADS

While biscuits and cornbread may reign as king and queen of Southern bread, there are many other important members of the family. Many local fruits and vegetables were mixed in with dough to create new breads. This was often done to take advantage of abundant seasonal harvests. For example, as anyone who has grown zucchini knows, it can become a struggle to find creative ways to use its prolific output. Also falling into the category of what we are calling "other" breads are many that originated in other countries but have been adapted over time to have unique Southern interpretations.

The beginnings and even the namesake of Sally Lunn bread are shrouded in mystery but can be traced back to at least Bath, England, in the 1700s. Some even say it came from France before that, which might be believable since it does have similarities to a brioche. Wherever it originated, Sally Lunn bread was brought to the South by English colonists, and here it became very popular, particularly in Virginia. In England, it is traditionally baked in a round shape, but across the Atlantic, it is more often made as a loaf. If you want to eat breakfast like a legendary president, try the Sally Lunn recipe; reports say it was a favorite of George Washington.

Other European groups brought popular bread traditions with them that have remained strong. In New Orleans and much of Louisiana, it was the French who greatly shaped the bread culture. From that country, we get baguettes, which are used for the famous po' boy sandwich. There are many variations along the Gulf coast, but they are often filled with fried oysters, fried shrimp or Cajun sausage and served on a crusty short baguette. The iconic muffuletta sandwich, served on round sesame bread, also comes from New Orleans, so many assume its origins are French as well. The truth, however, is that it was actually created by Italian immigrants, particularly those who arrived in large numbers from Sicily in the late 1800s.

Though the earliest settlers get most of the credit for establishing what would become Southern bread culture, more recent groups have continued to play a role.

A loaf of Sally Lunn bread cooling on the rack.

Since the 1980s, there has been a great increase in in the number of Mexicans migrating to the United States. They have spread far beyond the border states and taken their food traditions with them. Now, tamales, tortillas and other bread types from Mexico are popular across the South and enjoyed by people of all ethnicities.

The tamale is not a typical bread dish, but it does serve the same role in a meal. Tamales (and corn tortillas) are made through the process of nixtamalization, which begins with soaking and cooking the corn in an alkaline solution generally made up of slaked lime (calcium hydroxide) and ash (potassium hydroxide). This creates hominy, which is called masa when ground to flour consistency (coarsely ground hominy is used to make grits). Ground corn that is not treated in this way is unable to be transformed into dough when water is added. The process also increased the nutritional value of the corn by adding the essential vitamin niacin.

Tamales originated with the Native Americans of southern Mexico, but when the Spanish arrived, they adopted it and spread it with them. When Spanish colonization through missions spread north into Texas and Louisiana, the tradition of tamales went, too. It wasn't until much later, however, that tamales really gained wide exposure north of the border. Sometime around the 1920s, perhaps thanks to Mexican workers in the cotton fields, spicy "hot tamales" became popular with the African Americans of the Mississippi Delta. They even inspired a popular song, "They're Red Hot," by

Making tortillas in San Antonio, Texas, in 1939. *Photo by Russell Lee, Courtesy Library of Congress.*

bluesman Robert Johnson in 1936. Another example of foods being adapted and accepted by new cultures, these Delta-style tamales are different from their ancestors. They are made of grittier corn meal instead of masa, are usually spicy and are most often filled with pork.

Like the tamale, the tortilla is a form of unleavened bread that originated south of the border but now plays a large role in the food culture of the United States. Developed centuries before the Spanish arrived, the tortilla (which, in Spanish, means "small cake") is an essential part of many meals. Its popularity and versatility have helped it gain popularity even among those not of Latin American descent. Tacos and burritos are one very popular way in which they are served, with the tortilla serving the same role as a hamburger bun or sandwich bread. Of course, corn tortillas can also be cut up and fried to create immensely popular tortillas chips, but that is venturing into the realm of snack foods.

While the corn tortilla is the original, it was soon discovered that the wheat the Spanish brought with them could be used in the same way. Today, both styles are very popular, and purists debate over which is more appropriate for which dish. Visit a taco stand, or taquería, and you might get the question "*Harina o maíz* (flour or corn)?" Most Mexicans would choose the corn variety, but flour tortillas rule among the non-Hispanic diners of the South.

Texas-style barbecue restaurant offering, complete with a bread feast of Texas toast and hushpuppies.

Another example of a bread that originated south of the border and then migrated north is Cuban bread. The basis for the popular Cuban sandwich, this white bread is similar to the long loaves of French and Italian bread. The difference, however, is a unique baking method and ingredients, particularly the addition of a small amount of lard or vegetable shortening. It came to Florida with Cuban immigrants and soon became popular in places such as Tampa and Miami. Most agree that the first loaf of American-made Cuban bread was baked at La Joven Francesca Bakery in Tampa's Ybor City in 1896.

A last popular bread from the South deserving mention is Texas toast. The origins of this bread style, which is essentially just white loaf bread in thicker slices, are unknown, but credit often goes to the Pig Stand, a chain of barbecue restaurants that began in Dallas in the early 1920s. Supposedly, the first Texas toast was served at its Beaumont, Texas location around 1941. Too thick for the toaster, this toast was buttered on both sides and grilled. Its popularity grew, and today, it is a popular side (often in place of hushpuppies) with Texas-style barbecue, such as brisket, thanks to its ability to absorb extra sauce.

The evolution of Southern bread continues.

RICE IS (OR WAS) NICE

In the South Carolina Lowcountry and coastal Georgia, a crop that once thrived was rice. Before the Civil War, thanks especially to the labor of African slaves, it was plentiful. Wheat, on the other hand, was scarce and expensive. Rice could be ground or boiled and used in baking, but due to its density and lack of gluten, it did not rise in a normal bread-like manner. Often, the solution was to combine it with wheat flour to create breads with distinctive consistency and taste.

Today, rice is no longer a commercial crop in Georgia, and only a small amount is grown in South Carolina (most Southern production has shifted to Louisiana and Texas). Though rice bread may have essentially vanished, it does exist in many historic recipes. Charlestonian Sarah Rutledge included these recipes when she published *The Carolina Housewife* in 1847:

Rice culture on the Ogeechee, near Savannah, Georgia, around the time of the Civil War. *Courtesy Library of Congress.*

Potato and Rice Bread

One quart of rice flour, one table-spoonful of mashed sweet potatoe, one table-spoonful of butter, mixed with half a pint of yeast and a pint of milk. Bake in a pan, and in a moderate oven.

Beaufort Rice Bread

A pint of boiled rice, half a pint of hommony [*sic*], three pints of rice flour; mix with water enough to make a thick batter; add a tea-cup of yeast and a tea-spoonful of pearlash. Leave the mixture to rise for eight or ten hours, and bake in a deep pan.

Carolina Rice and Wheat Bread

Simmer one pound of rice in two quarts of water until it is quite soft; when it is cool enough, mix it well with four pounds of flour, yeast and salt as for other bread; of yeast, four large spoonfuls. Let it rise before the fire. Some of the flour should be reserved to make the loaves. If the rice swells greatly, and requires more water, add as much as you think proper.

Rice Biscuits

Boil soft half a pint of rice; when cold, add to it half a pint of rice flour, a spoonful of fresh butter, half a pint of milk, and sufficient salt. Mix all well together, and drop it in large spoonfuls on tin sheets in the oven. Bake till brown, and thoroughly.

CORNMEAL WAFFLES

Makes 4 waffles

WAFFLES
4 tablespoons butter, softened
1 egg
¾ cup buttermilk
1 cup all-purpose flour
2 tablespoons cornmeal
2 teaspoons baking powder
1 teaspoon baking soda
1 tablespoon sugar
¼ teaspoon salt

SORGHUM BUTTER
1 stick butter, softened
2 tablespoons sorghum

Beat butter with a hand mixer until light and fluffy. Add remaining ingredients and beat until just combined, scraping down the sides of the bowl several times.

For butter, combine butter and sorghum and set aside.

Cook in a hot waffle maker until golden on both sides. Serve warm with fried chicken and sorghum butter.

•••••

FRIED CHICKEN

Fried chicken is the perfect Southern addition to waffles!

1 whole chicken, cut into 8 pieces, or 3 breasts, divided into 9 pieces and pounded slightly

2 cups buttermilk

2 tablespoons hot sauce, or more to taste

salt and pepper, to taste

2 eggs

1½ cups flour

2 tablespoons all-purpose seasoning blend

1½ cups panko

grapeseed or neutral oil, for frying

Place chicken in large zipper-lock plastic bag and add buttermilk and hot sauce. Remove most of the air and seal tightly. Place in a shallow pan and refrigerate at least 4 hours or overnight.

Preheat oven to 350 degrees. Remove chicken and place on a rack on a baking sheet. Let drain slightly. Season with salt and pepper.

Pour leftover buttermilk from marinade into a shallow bowl and whisk in eggs. Place flour, seasoning mix and panko in a shallow pan and whisk. Dip chicken pieces in flour, then egg mixture and flour again and return to the rack.

Heat oil 1 inch deep in a cast-iron skillet until oil is shimmering and bubbles vigorously when the end of a wooden spoon is inserted (350 degrees). Cook chicken in batches until nicely browned on all sides. Place the chicken on a clean rack over a baking pan with shallow sides. Once chicken is browned on all sides place in the oven and cook for 30 to 40 minutes, until cooked through. The internal temperature should be 165 degrees.

•••••

BUTTERMILK PANCAKES

These pancakes are a family favorite. We don't have pancakes very often, but when we do, these are so fluffy and delicious. Heating the jam, jelly or syrup is a welcome addition.

—Marilyn Markel

Serves 4

1 cup flour
2 tablespoons sugar
2 tablespoons baking powder
½ teaspoon salt
1 egg
1 cup buttermilk
3 tablespoons oil or bacon grease
softened butter, for finished pancakes
syrup or jam (any kind)

Whisk together the flour, sugar, baking powder and salt. Whisk together the egg and buttermilk. Heat oil on medium in a cast-iron or other skillet. Pour buttermilk mixture into the flour mixture and stir with a spatula to combine.

Drop by ¼-cup measure into hot oil. When the top forms large pockets, turn and cook on the other side for several minutes.

Keep in a warm oven until ready to serve. Heat syrup or jam over low heat until ready to serve.

ZUCCHINI PANCAKES WITH COUNTRY HAM AND BUTTERMILK CRÈME FRAÎCHE

These make a lot of small pancakes perfect for an appetizer portion. They are delicious at room temperature on a platter with a bowl of the crème fraîche and a garnish of country ham or smoked trout.

—Marilyn Markel

Serves 6–8

1 pound grated zucchini, stems removed
1 heaping teaspoon salt
2 tablespoons finely chopped chives, plus additional for garnish

1 shallot, minced
¼ teaspoon pepper
¼ cup flour
1 egg
¼ cup neutral oil
2 ounces thinly sliced country ham or smoked trout (optional)
½ cup crème fraîche (optional), recipe follows

Combine zucchini and salt in a colander and let sit over a sink or bowl for a half hour. Squeeze zucchini dry and press dry onto paper towels or a smooth, clean dishtowel.

Combine zucchini with chives, shallot, pepper, flour and egg in a medium bowl.

Heat oil in a skillet on medium. Drop zucchini pancakes into oil by heaping tablespoons. Cook for several minutes per side and keep warm while cooking remaining pancakes, adding more oil as necessary. Serve with crème fraîche, chives and smoked trout or salmon.

BUTTERMILK CRÈME FRAÎCHE

Makes 1 cup

4 tablespoons buttermilk
1 cup heavy cream

If making your own crème fraîche, combine the buttermilk and cream in a small jar. Tightly screw on the lid. Shake vigorously and let sit at room temperature for about 36 hours, until it's the consistency of thick yogurt. Refrigerate until ready to use.

When I was growing up in Alabama we had help around the house but not to do the cooking. That was my mother's territory. When it came to breads it was just something she did all the time. Cornbread, biscuits, banana nut bread and so on—she did it all, and she did it by memory. And because she loved it so much, I never really learned to make breads myself. She did let me cut out biscuits, but that was about it. Since she never wrote anything down, we had a devil of a time years later trying to figure out how she made her cornbread stuffing!

—Susan Frankenberg

SAVORY APPLE PANCAKES WITH BACON TOPPING

Apples are abundant in the late summer in the South. Great apples from a local farmers' market or orchard are a good choice. They often look rustic, but they have delicious flavor and do not contain wax as some of the supermarket varieties do.

—Marilyn Markel

Makes about 30 2-inch pancakes

2 tablespoons olive oil, divided

2 apples, peeled, seeded and chopped

2 medium shallots, minced (about ¼ cup)

2 cloves garlic

½ teaspoon minced fresh thyme

2 eggs

1 cup grated sharp cheddar

¼ cup all-purpose flour

¼ cup whole wheat flour

1 tablespoon maple syrup

pinch cayenne

4 slices bacon, cooked and finely minced

crème fraiche (optional), for serving, see page 105

Heat 1 tablespoon olive oil over medium in a medium skillet until sizzling. Add apples and shallots and cook until softened. Add garlic and thyme and cook for another minute. Remove from the skillet and cool.

Lightly beat eggs in a bowl. Add the cooled apple mixture, cheese and the flours. Add additional flour if needed for the batter to hold together.

Heat the remaining olive oil over medium heat and scoop out pancakes in heaping tablespoons. Cook until brown on one side. Flip and flatten slightly. Drain. Continue cooking in batches until all the batter is used.

Combine maple syrup, cayenne and bacon in a small ovenproof dish. Cook until mixture is loosened up and nicely browned. Turn down oven to warm or off.

Place pancakes on a serving dish and top each pancake with a little maple-bacon mixture. Serve with crème fraîche on the side, if desired.

I have bread with almost every meal. I love bread. Big cathead biscuits and small cathead biscuits—regardless of what size they are, they are all good. We eat them with white gravy. I love them; it's just what I was brought up with. We'd fix gravy and eggs and sausage or bacon, and we'd take that gravy and put that over them biscuits. I've had homemade biscuits all my life. Another favorite of mine is cornbread, like my wife makes. Now cornbread in the South is a lot different than [it is] anywhere else. We use white cornmeal, not yellow, and it's like a dessert. After I eat my cornbread with my regular meal, sometimes I take an extra piece, and as long as it's good and hot, you take a good piece of butter and let it melt down in the cornbread. And you take a fork and cut into that cornbread with butter—it's better than dessert.

I like good rolls, too, sometimes, but I try to limit myself to cornbread and cathead biscuits. When you're in the South, you have to have it—cathead biscuits for breakfast and cornbread for supper. There's an offshoot of cornbread we do, too, called fritters. Get your skillet hot, then take the same cornbread mix and pour it in, about the size of a small pancake. Fry it, flip it and cover it with butter. It's so good. They go good with beans. Sometimes we put corn, onion and peños in the mix and fry them. We just add whatever we like for our tastes, sometime just the onions. You can spice it up many different ways by adding a few ingredients, but it's all good.

—Larry Flanary

PEA AND CORN CAKES WITH SUN-DRIED TOMATOES

Serves 6–8

2 cups summer peas, cleaned, boiled in water until tender and drained

2 cups corn kernels, preferably fresh off the cob

¼ cup minced red bell peppers

¼ cup minced sun-dried tomatoes in oil

1 teaspoon salt

½ teaspoon pepper

⅔ cup flour

2 eggs

2 tablespoons canola oil

Combine peas, corn, red pepper, sun-dried tomatoes, salt, pepper, flour and eggs.

Heat oil in a cast-iron skillet. Place a spoonful of the mixture into the heated pan. Flatten slightly with a spatula. Cook until golden and flip the pancakes. Repeat. Add more oil, if necessary.

ICE-BOX CRESCENT ROLLS

We are not sure of the origin of this recipe, probably a *Southern Living* magazine circa the 1960s or '70s, but my mother-in-law has made them for years for Thanksgiving. She would pack them up and send them home with us along with some leftover turkey. We would enjoy these delicious after-Thanksgiving leftover sandwiches every year with a slathering of Durkee's Famous Sauce.

—Marilyn Markel

Makes 2 dozen

1 package instant yeast
4 cups warm water
4½ to 5 cups all-purpose flour
½ cup sugar
1 teaspoon salt
¾ cup butter, softened
2 eggs
¾ cup warm milk

Dissolve yeast in warm water.

Combine 4½ cups flour, sugar and salt in a large mixing bowl. Cut in ¾ cup butter with pastry blender until mixture resembles coarse meal.

Combine eggs, milk and yeast mixture and add to flour, stirring well. Dough will be sticky. Cover dough and refrigerate overnight.

Punch dough down and divide in half.

Roll each half into a 12-inch circle and divide into 12 wedges. Roll up each wedge tightly beginning at the wide end. Seal points and place rolls, point side down, on greased or parchment-lined baking sheets. Curve rolls into crescent shapes. Brush with melted butter. Cover rolls and let rise about an hour or so until doubled in volume.

Preheat oven to 400 degrees. Bake for 10 minutes, until nicely browned. Brush with additional butter, if desired.

FROG MUFFINS

I was unfamiliar with FROG jelly until recent years. It's a delicious combination of fig, raspberry, orange and ginger. If FROG jelly is delicious why not FROG muffins?

—Marilyn Markel

Makes 12

1 stick butter, softened
¾ cup sugar
2 eggs
1 cup buttermilk
1 teaspoon vanilla
2 cups all-purpose flour
½ teaspoon salt
¾ teaspoon baking soda
1 tablespoon baking powder

2 tablespoons minced dried figs

1 cup sliced raspberries

2 teaspoons orange zest

1 tablespoon minced crystallized ginger

Preheat oven to 375 degrees. Line a standard muffin tin with cupcake liners.

Combine the butter and sugar in a large bowl and beat with a handheld electric mixer until smooth. Combine the eggs with the buttermilk, add the vanilla and whisk.

Combine the flour, salt, baking soda and baking powder in a small bowl and whisk well.

Add ⅓ of the buttermilk mixture to the butter-sugar mixture and stir well with a spatula. Add ½ of the flour mixture and stir just until combined. Add another ⅓ of buttermilk mixture and stir. Repeat with remaining flour and buttermilk mixture. Stir in fruit, zest and ginger.

Divide equally into prepared or lined muffin tins and bake about 15 minutes or so, until cake tester comes out clean.

●◆●◆●

PEACH BREAD

This is delicious on its own or served with a slathering of whipped cream cheese and peach jam. Peaches are abundant in the South in the summer, and we are always looking for creative ways to devour them.

—Marilyn Markel

Makes 1 9-inch loaf

1 stick soft butter, plus 2 tablespoons

1 cup honey

1 teaspoon cinnamon

1 teaspoon vanilla

2½ cups self-rising flour

½ cup buttermilk

3 eggs

2 cups chopped peaches, peeled and pitted

¾ cup chopped pecans, toasted

1 cup whipped cream cheese (optional)

½ cup peach jam (optional)

Preheat oven to 350 degrees. Cream the stick of butter. Add honey, cinnamon and vanilla. Beat well.

Add half the flour and mix. Add half the buttermilk and mix. Mix in remaining flour and buttermilk. Add eggs one at a time and mix well. Stir in the peaches and pecans.

Pour into a 9-inch loaf pan and bake for a 1½ hours, until tester comes out clean.

—◦•◦—

GRIT CAKES WITH HOT PEPPER JELLY

Serves 8

1 recipe of grits, recipe follows
1 tablespoon butter
oil or duck fat
1 cup flour
salt
6 ounces country ham, cut into pieces

1 jar hot pepper jelly, for serving
4 green onions, green parts only, chopped

Cook grits according to recipe that follows. Butter a 9 by 9 square pan and add cooked grits. Cool to room temperature, cover and chill overnight or up to 3 days.

Preheat oven to 300 degrees.

Cut grits into squares (or any shape). Add 1 inch oil or fat to a skillet and heat fat over medium until it bubbles vigorously when the handle of a wooden spoon is inserted. Dip grit cakes into flour. Brush off the excess. Cook in hot oil until nicely browned on the first side (about 10 minutes). Turn the cake over and cook for about 5 minutes on the second side. Place on a drying rack over a sheet pan. Sprinkle with salt. Keep warm in the oven until remaining cakes are cooked.

Heat a little fat in the skillet. Sauté the country ham until crispy.

Heat jelly in a small saucepan on low heat until warmed through.

Serve immediately with jam drizzled on top and garnished with green onions.

GRITS

Makes 4 cups

2 cups water
½ cup stone-ground grits
¾ cup milk, plus extra if needed
salt and pepper, to taste
2 tablespoons butter

Bring the water to a gentle boil in a medium saucepan. Slowly stir in the grits, whisking constantly. Add a pinch of salt.

Reduce heat to a simmer and continue cooking, whisking frequently, for about 45 minutes, or until the grits are thick and tender. The longer you cook them, the creamier they will get. You will need to add milk as grits thicken.

Stir in salt, pepper and butter.

HOT AND SWEET MULTI-PEPPER JELLY

Makes 10 half-pint jars

1 red bell pepper, stemmed, seeded and chopped
½ cup stemmed, seeded and chopped jalapeños
½ cup stemmed, seeded and chopped banana peppers
1¼ cups white vinegar
4 cups sugar
1 pouch pectin

Pulse peppers in a food processor until finely chopped. Can also chop by hand or use an old-fashioned food grinder.

Bring the vinegar and sugar to a boil and cook until sugar is dissolved. Add the peppers and cook for a couple of minutes, skimming off any foam.

Add the pectin and boil for 1 minute. Remove and skim foam again. Put into sterilized jars, process for 5 minutes in a hot-water bath or store in the refrigerator.

ALL-PURPOSE BUNS

This is an all-purpose sandwich bread that can be used for the famed muffulettas from New Orleans or hamburgers, that all-American cuisine. For the Fourth of July or a child's birthday party, hamburgers are a family staple. Try making your own buns and Brinkley Farm pork burgers with bread-and-butter pickles for our take on this classic. These rolls also make dinner buns or sliders. Just divide into sixteen pieces instead of eight.

—Marilyn Markel

Makes 8 buns

3 cups flour
1 tablespoon sugar
1 heaping teaspoon instant yeast
1 heaping teaspoon kosher salt
1 cup milk
1 tablespoon bacon grease or oil
1 to 2 tablespoons seeds, such as sesame or poppy

Add the flour, sugar, yeast and salt to the bowl of an electric mixer. Add the dough hook and stir on lowest speed. Add the milk and grease and place on medium speed for 2 minutes. Turn off mixer and let rest for 10 minutes.

Turn mixer back to medium and stir for another 2 minutes or until dough is smooth and elastic.

Form dough into a nice ball and place in an oiled bowl. Cover with a towel and refrigerate overnight or up to 2 days.

Turn the dough out onto a lightly floured surface and, using a dough scraper, divide the dough into 8 equal pieces. It's easiest to divide dough into half 4 times. Carefully form each piece into a ball and place on a parchment-lined sheet pan, or as you cut, just make squares. Hamburgers can be square, too. Flatten slightly.

Allow dough to rise about 3 hours or more, until doubled in size.

Preheat the oven to 450 degrees. Lightly spray buns with water and sprinkle with any seeds, if using. Use sesame seeds if making muffulettas.

Reduce heat to 425 degrees and bake rolls for 15 to 20 minutes, until internal temperatures reach 200 degrees.

MUFFULETTA

Serves 8

4 ounces mortadella, thinly sliced

4 ounces ham, thinly sliced

4 ounces salami, thinly sliced

4 ounces provolone, thinly sliced

4 ounces smoked mozzarella, thinly sliced

1 cup green pimento-stuffed olives, roughly chopped

¼ cup Kalamata olives, roughly chopped

1 clove garlic, minced

¼ cup finely chopped piquillo peppers or roasted red pepper

2 tablespoons chopped parsley

¼ cup finely chopped celery

¼ cup chopped pepperoncini

1 teaspoon oregano

¼ cup olive oil

2 tablespoons red wine vinegar

salt and pepper, to taste
8 All-Purpose Buns (page 113)

Cut meats and cheeses in sizes that will fit bread.

Beginning with green olives, combine all ingredients in a bowl and stir. This may be made a couple of days ahead and refrigerated.

Cut 8 sandwich rolls in half. Spread one half generously with olive mixture, add divided meats and cheeses and top with second half of bread. Serve.

BRINKLEY'S FAMOUS PORK BURGERS

The Brinkleys have amazing vegetables and meat products they sell at a couple of North Carolina farmers' markets. They joined me to teach a class and brought the idea of this amazing burger to us. Check your local market or butcher for this type of meat. Try this on the Fourth of July or any occasion that calls for a cookout!

—Marilyn Markel

Serves 8

2 ounces ground or minced country ham
2 pounds ground pork
salt and pepper, to taste
4 ounces blue cheese
Dijon mustard, to taste

Combine the pork and the country ham. Form into 8 patties. Season to taste. Pan fry in a little oil, turning once, until cooked to desired doneness, or grill on a hot grill.

Serve on hamburger buns with crumbled blue cheese, bread-and-butter pickles and mustard.

BREAD-AND-BUTTER PICKLES

This pickle recipe is from my friend Margie's mom in Texas. It's fabulous and easy to make. Make them in the summer when all the cucumbers are local and abundant throughout the South. They are a requirement for a good burger or sandwich!

—Marilyn Markel

Makes 5–6 pints

25 pickling cucumbers, sliced thickly
2 white onions, sliced
2 red bell peppers, seeded and sliced
¼ cup kosher salt
2½ cups sugar
2½ cups white vinegar
2 teaspoons kosher salt
2 teaspoons mustard seed
2 teaspoons turmeric
2 teaspoons celery seed

Place the sliced cucumbers, onions and red peppers in a large cooler with ice and toss with salt. Set aside for at least four hours. Drain and rinse vegetables. Pack the vegetables in large, sterile jars.

Bring the remaining ingredients to a boil. Pour the boiling mixture over the vegetables and proceed with canning the jars. Process in a hot-water bath for 15 minutes. Let sit one month before opening.

SALLY LUNN BREAD

Makes 1 loaf

1¾ cups flour
3 tablespoons sugar
½ teaspoon salt
½ cup milk
4 tablespoons butter
¼ cup warm water
1 teaspoon instant yeast
1 egg
1 egg yolk

Combine the flour, sugar and salt. Whisk briefly.

Heat the milk and butter in a saucepan over medium heat until the butter melts. Add the water and yeast and whisk to combine. Allow to sit 5 minutes. Add the eggs and beat lightly.

Stir the liquid ingredients into the dry mixture and stir with a spatula until all ingredients are incorporated. Put bowl in the refrigerator overnight or up to 2 days. About 2 hours before you're ready to bake, remove the dough from the refrigerator.

Pour into a buttered 9-inch loaf pan.

Preheat oven to 400 degrees. After the dough rises until doubled in height, put the loaf into the oven and reduce temperature to 375 degrees. Bake for about 45 minutes, until internal temperature reaches 190 to 200 degrees. Cool on a rack. When cool, run a knife down the edges of the pan and turn the loaf out onto a rack.

MOLASSES BUTTER

1 stick butter, softened
1 tablespoon good-quality molasses
¼ teaspoon smoked sea salt

Combine the butter, molasses and salt. Taste and add salt, if needed. Serve with warm bread.

To shape into a log, drop by large spoonfuls onto the center of a piece of parchment or wax paper. Leave about 4 inches on either side and 6 inches on the bottom. Fold the top of the paper over the butter and secure with a sharp-edged pan. Pull the bottom 6 inches while holding the pan against the butter. As you pull the paper and hold the butter in place with the pan, the butter will be rolled into a cylinder about 6 inches longer than when you began. This will make a nice, tight log. Refrigerate until ready to use.

PARMESAN AND HERB COMPOUND BUTTER

1 stick butter, softened
½ cup grated Parmesan cheese
2 cloves garlic, grated
2 tablespoons minced chives
2 tablespoons minced parsley
¼ teaspoon ground black pepper
½ teaspoon salt, or more to taste

Combine the butter, Parmesan, garlic, chives, parsley and pepper. Taste and add salt, if needed. Serve with warm bread.

COUNTRY HAM COMPOUND BUTTER

1 stick butter, softened
1 very thin slice country ham, diced
1 tablespoons chives, minced

Combine butter, country ham and chives in a bowl.

To shape into a log, drop by large spoonfuls onto the center of a piece of parchment or wax paper. Leave about 4 inches on either side and 6 inches on the bottom. Fold the top of the paper over the butter and secure with a sharp-edged pan. Pull the bottom 6 inches while holding the pan against the butter.

As you pull the paper and hold the butter in place with the pan, the butter will be rolled into a cylinder about 6 inches longer than when you began.

Chill until ready to use. May be frozen for up to a month.

ROASTED RADISH BRUSCHETTA WITH COMPOUND CHIVE BUTTER

1 bunch radishes
drizzle olive oil, plus additional
salt and pepper, to taste
4 thick slices Sally Lunn Bread (page 117)
4 ounces butter
½ teaspoon minced garlic
1 tablespoon minced chives
coarse sea salt or fleur de sel with espellette, to taste

Preheat oven to 375 degrees. Trim and rinse radishes and toss with olive oil, salt and pepper. Place in baking pan and roast for 30 to 45 minutes, until you can easily pierce the radishes with a sharp knife.

Remove and slice.

Brush bread with olive oil. Sprinkle with salt and pepper and bake until crisp, about 5 to 10 minutes.

Combine butter, garlic, chives and salt.

Brush herbed butter on bread and top with sliced, roasted radishes. Store remaining butter in the refrigerator.

HEIRLOOM MULTICOLORED TOMATO SALAD

1 pound assorted fresh heirloom tomatoes
1 clove garlic, boiled for 1 minute
1 small bunch basil, julienned
1 teaspoon lemon zest
2 tablespoons olive oil
dash balsamic vinegar
salt and freshly ground pepper, to taste

Core the tomatoes and slice them.

Dice or smash the garlic and add to the tomatoes. Add the basil and lemon zest.

Add olive oil and balsamic vinegar. Season with salt and pepper.

HEIRLOOM TOMATO SANDWICHES WITH HOMEMADE MAYONNAISE

Makes approximately 1 cup of mayonnaise

2 tablespoons lemon juice
1 teaspoon hot sauce, or more to taste
1 egg yolk
pinch sugar

½ teaspoon salt
¾ cup grapeseed or canola oil
2 pounds heirloom tomatoes, various colors and shapes
8 slices Sally Lunn Bread (page 117), toasted or grilled

In a blender or food processor, add lemon juice, hot sauce, egg yolk, sugar and salt. Blend. On low speed, very slowly in a thin stream, add oil. Mixture will become thick and glossy.

Slice tomatoes and arrange on plate or platter with bread. Place mayonnaise in a bowl to pass around table.

BREAKFAST CINNAMON BUNS WITH SORGHUM BUTTER

Makes 9

BUNS

½ cup buttermilk

2 tablespoons butter, softened

2 teaspoons instant yeast

1 egg

2¼ cups flour

2 tablespoons brown sugar

½ teaspoon salt

FILLING

3 tablespoons butter, softened

2 teaspoons cinnamon

¼ cup sugar

1 tablespoon cream

GLAZE

2 ounces cream cheese, softened

2 tablespoons butter, softened

1 tablespoon sorghum

½ cup confectioner's sugar

½ teaspoon vanilla extract

Heat the buttermilk and butter in a small saucepan or the microwave. When cool enough to touch, add yeast and egg and whisk. In a separate bowl, combine flour, brown sugar and salt.

Add the liquid ingredients into the bowl with the flour mixture. Stir with a spatula until the dough forms a ball. Place the dough on a lightly floured surface and knead, incorporating flour as needed for 10 minutes, or until dough is smooth. Form the dough into a ball and place it in an oiled bowl. Turned the dough once and cover with plastic for 1½ to 2 hours, until dough is more than doubled in bulk.

After dough is proofed, turn it out onto a lightly floured surface and roll out to an 8- by 12-inch rectangle. Dot the dough all over with soft butter, spreading it over the surface with you finger. Combine the cinnamon and sugar. Sprinkle the entire surface of the dough with the cinnamon sugar.

Spread a little cream on the far outer edge with you finger. Roll the 12-inch side over into a tight roll. Press the seam in by pinching the edge. With the seam side down, cut the dough with a serrated knife into 12 equal pieces. Place each piece with a spiral side up into a buttered 9-inch square pan.

Cover and let rise for an hour or in the refrigerator overnight.

If rising in the refrigerator, remove from the refrigerator and let rise for 1 hour before baking. Preheat the oven to 350 degrees. Bake for about 30 minutes, until rolls are golden.

With a handheld mixer beat the cream cheese, butter and sorghum until light and fluffy. Add the confectioner's sugar and vanilla and beat until smooth.

When the rolls are nicely browned remove from the oven and brush with the glaze while they are still warm. Serve either warm or at room temperature.

CORN TORTILLAS

Makes 24

2 cups masa
½ teaspoon salt
1½ cups water

Combine masa and salt in a medium bowl. With a spatula stir in water. Using your hands knead the dough until all is incorporated. The dough should not be sticky. You can adjust masa/water to make dough smooth.

Pinch off dough by heaping tablespoons and press out lightly. Roll out into a thin circle or press with a plastic wrap–lined tortilla press.

Heat skillet on medium heat. Cook tortillas in dry skillet one at a time.

FLOUR TORTILLAS

Makes 12

2 cups flour
1 teaspoon salt
3 tablespoons lard or shortening
½ cup water

Combine flour and salt in a medium bowl. Add lard and incorporate completely into flour using your fingertips or a pastry blender. With a spatula, stir in water. Using your hands, knead the dough until all is incorporated. The dough should not be sticky. You can adjust flour/water to make dough smooth.

Form into a ball. Cover the ball with a dishtowel and let rest one hour. Divide dough into 12 equal balls. Roll out balls into 7-inch disks.

Heat skillet over medium heat and cook for about 1 minute on each side, until lightly browned and bubbled slightly.

DUCK CONFIT TACOS

Serves 4

2 cooked duck confit legs
½ pound Yukon gold potatoes, chopped
canola oil, as needed
1 small onion, chopped
4 piquillo peppers, drained and chopped
¼ teaspoon chili powder, or more to taste
salt and pepper, to taste
8 flour or corn tortillas
Salsa Cruda, recipe follows

Remove fat from duck legs. Dice into small pieces and reserve. Pick over duck meat and remove any bones/sinew.

Bring a small saucepan of water to a boil. Boil potatoes until almost cooked through. Drain.

Heat oil in a medium skillet until shimmering. Add the duck fat and cook until crispy. Remove with a slotted spoon. Add duck pieces and cook until crispy. Remove with a slotted spoon.

Add additional oil, if needed. Cook onion, until softened. Add potatoes and cook until lightly browned. Add piquillos, duck and duck fat pieces. Season with chili powder, salt and pepper.

Serve on warmed tortillas with Salsa Cruda (recipe follows).

SALSA CRUDA

The options for salsa ingredients are unlimited, and it is such a versatile condiment. It is also a great way to use up extra summer vegetables from your garden. This is a basic one I think is delicious as it is, but don't be afraid to experiment!

4 summer tomatoes, finely chopped
½ white onion, finely chopped
2 jalapeño peppers, minced
½ cup chopped fresh cilantro
squirt lime juice
coarse salt

Combine all ingredients. This benefits from sitting at room temperature for an hour.

Knowing how to make good Southern bread was even important to the war effort. Here, Cooks and Bakers School students practice their skills at the U.S. Maritime Service Training Station in St. Petersburg, Florida, in 1943. *Courtesy Library of Congress.*

OTHER OLDIES

SWEET POTATO BUNS

Boil and mash a potato, rub into it as much flour as will make it like bread—add spice and sugar to your taste. With a spoonful of yeast; when it has risen well, work in a piece of butter, bake it in small roll, to be eaten hot with butter, either for breakfast or tea.

—from *The Virginia Housewife*, 1838

MISS SHATTUCK'S BROWN BREAD

One quart of rye meal, two quarts of Indian meal, two tablespoons of molasses; mix thoroughly with sweet milk. Let it stand for two hours, and bake in a slow oven.

—from *La Cuisine Creole*, 1885

SALLY LUNN

Pour a cup of risen yeast into a bowl, add a cup of warm sweet milk, one-half a cup of white sugar, and a large spoonful each of lard and butter mixed and warmed; also add four eggs well beaten, three and one-half cups of sifted flour, and a little salt. Beat all this well, and pour into a warm and well-greased cake pan and set it to rise in a warm place in winter, and a cool place in summer. If you wish it for tea, make it up five hours beforehand, having set the yeast to rise after breakfast. If wanted for breakfast, make it up at nine o'clock the night before. Remember if made up at night, you add a little more flour, or make the dough a little stiffer, and do not put it in a pan at night, but allow it to rise in a tureen or crock, and pour it in a pan and let it rise a little before baking. It must be baked like a cake. This is a never failing recipe and has been much liked.

—from *La Cuisine Creole*, 1885

GERMAN RUSKS

1 quart of flour.
2 eggs.
2 cups of sugar.
2 cups of lard and butter mixed.
2 cups of potato yeast.
2 cups of milk.
1 nutmeg.

Put all the ingredients in the middle of the flour, work well together and set to rise as loaf bread. Wash the rolls over with butter and sugar.

—from *Housekeeping in Old Virginia*, 1878

OLD VIRGINIA LOAF BREAD

Boil one large Irish potato, until well done, then peel and mash it fine, adding a little cold water to soften it. Stir into it

1 teaspoonful of brown sugar.
1 tablespoonful of sweet lard.

Then add three tablespoonfuls of good hop yeast.
Mix the ingredients thoroughly, then put the sponge [Note: sponge is a word for dough raised with yeast, especially before kneading] in a mug with a close-fitting top, and let it stand several hours to rise.

Sift into the tray three pints of the best family flour, to which add a teaspoonful of salt. Then pour in the sponge and add enough cold water to the flour to work it up into a rather stiff dough. Knead it till the dough is smooth, then let it stand all night to rise. Work it over in the morning, using just enough flour to keep it from sticking to the hands. Allow it one hour to rise before baking and one hour to bake in a moderate oven. Then it will be thoroughly done and well dried.

Use a little lard on the hands when making out the loaf, as it keeps the crust from being too hard.

—from *Housekeeping in Old Virginia*, 1878

GRIDDLE CAKES

One and one-half cups of stale bread crumbs.
Two cups of milk.
One tablespoonful of butter.
One teaspoonful of salt.
One-half cupful of flour.

Scald milk and pour over bread crumbs. Beat two eggs well together, then add salt, milk and bread crumbs, flour and lastly the melted lard or butter.

—from *Aunt Caroline's Dixieland Recipes*, 1922

Chapter 7

FOLLOWING THE INSTRUCTIONS

Cooking has evolved as technology has improved and tastes have changed. Ovens are better and more accurate, ingredients are more widely available and flavors that were once limited to certain regions have spread due to increased ease of travel.

The other big change is the recipe. What was once often only a paragraph of general information on how to make a dish is now a list of measured ingredients and organized directions. Culinary education is a huge business, and to help people learn to cook, recipes that allow students to accurately re-create dishes are crucial. This is true in all areas of cooking, but baking relies on precision—precise measurements, precise temperatures and precise cooking times. These have all been determined and recorded with countless tests.

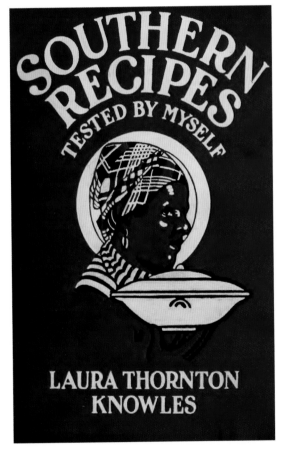

SOUTHERN RECIPES TESTED BY MYSELF

LAURA THORNTON KNOWLES

Though times and tastes change, old recipes can teach us much about how food has evolved in the American South. Since they are no longer bound by copyrights, many old cookbooks in which these recipes were assembled can be found for free on the Internet. Michigan State University—while definitely non-Southern—has a huge collection of American cookbooks that are available for free download. Below are some of the books we found most interesting while researching Southern bread heritage.

Aunt Caroline's Dixieland Recipes, Emma and William McKinney, 1922.

The Carolina Housewife, Sarah Rutledge, 1847

Cooking in Old Créole Days: La Cuisine Créole À L'Usage Des Petits Ménages, Célestine Eustis, 1904.

Dishes & Beverages of the Old South, Martha McCulloch-Williams, 1913.

Dixie Cookery; or, How I Managed My Table for Twelve Years: A Practical Cook-book for Southern Housekeepers, Maria Massey Barringer, 1867.

Echoes of Southern Kitchens, United Daughters of the Confederacy, California Division, Robert E. Lee Chapter, No. 278, Los Angeles, 1916.

Hints from Southern Epicures, Flower Committee of the Independent Presbyterian Church of Savannah, Georgia, 1892.

Housekeeping in Old Virginia, Containing Contributions from Two Hundred and Fifty Ladies in Virginia and Her Sister States, Distinguished for Their Skill in the Culinary Art, Marion Cabell Tyree, 1878.

La Cuisine Creole: A Collection of Culinary Recipes, from Leading Chefs and Noted Creole Housewives, Who Have Made New Orleans Famous for Its Cuisine, Lafcadio Hearn, 1885.

Rumford Southern Recipes, Mary A. Wilson, 1920.

The Southern Cook Book of Fine Old Recipes, edited by Lillie S. Lustig, S. Claire Sondheim and Sarah Rensel, 1935.

Southern Recipes, Tested by Myself, Laura Thornton Knowles, 1913.

A well-used 1961 copy of *Charleston Receipts* along with community cookbooks produced by the Junior League of Baton Rouge (left) and the Garden Club of Montgomery, Alabama. Produced as a way to raise funds for various charitable organizations, the first cookbooks in this category appeared around the time of the Civil War. Now, from all across the South, books such these preserve and document treasured family recipes that might not otherwise ever be shared.

Virginia Cookery-Book, Mary Stuart Smith, 1885.

The Virginia Housewife; or, Methodical Cook, Mary Randolph, 1838.

Beginning with these historic works, the list of cookbooks devoted to the art of Southern cooking is long today. Works by restaurant chefs, food historians and even television stars all contribute to the canon but leading the way has been the myriad spiral-bound community cookbooks put out by churches, schools and various organizations.

Perhaps the most successful of all of these, one that has taken on a life all its own, is *Charleston Receipts*. First published by the Junior League of Charleston in 1950, the collection of over four hundred recipes—many of them never before published—can now be found on kitchen shelves everywhere. The Lee brothers, who are authors and food experts passionate about Southern culinary traditions, even called *Charleston Receipts* "the definitive twentieth century cookbook" for the region.

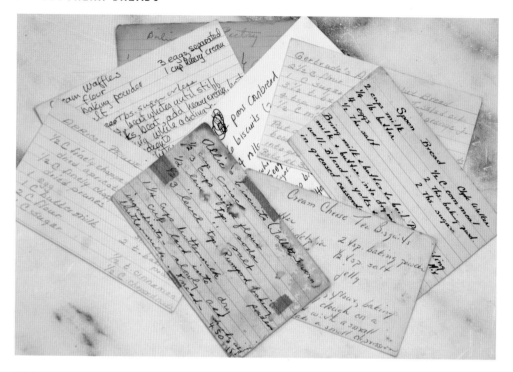

While some recipes make it into print in cookbooks, many exist only on faded and stained three- by five-inch cards. Often collected in boxes (or maybe just stuffed in kitchen drawers), these favorite recipes are traded, shared and passed down from generation to generation.

The book actually has an interesting history. In 1948, two younger members of the Junior League, Martha Lynch Humphreys and Margaret B. Walker, compiled family recipes for a book they called *Charleston Recipes*. They published 2,000 copies, which apparently sold well enough to catch the attention of more senior members of their group. Led by Mary Vereen Huguenin and Anne Montague Stoney, the Junior League of Charleston made revisions to the book, sought and tested new recipes and changed the cover from red to the now famous green. Using the old-fashioned word *receipts* instead of recipes in the title, they published 2,000 copies in 1950. It reportedly sold out in less than a week. The following year, they went through three print runs. Now, with somewhere in the neighborhood of 750,000 copies sold, the spiral-bound tome is almost required reading for every self-respecting cook.

Another regional book with enormous success from about the same time is *Marion Brown's Southern Cookbook*. A journalist and editor who lived in Burlington, North Carolina, Brown chronicled Southern cooking history and produced an invaluable culinary reference. First published in 1951, it has passed the half million mark in books sold and is still being printed by University of North Carolina Press.

Cookbooks from all across the rest of the South—from Texas to Chesapeake Bay—helped shape the culture of regional cuisine during the second half of the twentieth century, often with a focus on specific locales. From the big sellers by national publishers to the local books with small print runs, all of these recipe collections are a treasure to cooks. Flip through the pages and discover countless forgotten yet creative recipes. For example, when Alline Van Duzor retired from her position as director of the University Club of Tuscaloosa, Alabama, in 1961, she published *Fascinating Foods from the Deep South*, a cookbook filled with the recipes that had brought her local fame. Among them were her takes on many popular breads, but one that stands out is Peanut Butter Drop Biscuits. It uses a basic drop biscuit recipe with two cups of flour, to which she added four tablespoons of peanut butter to the dry mixture before shortening was added. She cooked them at 400 rather than 450 due to the peanut butter causing more rapid browning. It is a simple change to a Southern staple but interesting and tasty nonetheless.

The next time you pass a yard sale, stop and browse. You just might just be lucky enough to come across a few vintage cookbook treasures to add to your recipe collection.

RECIPE INDEX

ABOUT THE AUTHORS

MARILYN MARKEL

One of the top culinary instructors in the South, Marilyn has pursued her passion for teaching in Dallas, Texas; Chapel Hill, North Carolina; and the Charleston, South Carolina area, where she now resides. The Georgia native has taught countless classes on all aspects of cooking and served as culinary director for several schools. Marilyn is a member of Les Dames d'Escoffier, Southern Foodways Alliance and International Association of Culinary Professionals (IACP). Her work has appeared in the *Charleston Post and Courier*, among other newspapers, and the magazine *Edible Piedmont*, and she was featured in the documentary *Pimento Cheese, Please*, produced by the Southern Foodways Alliance.

CHRIS HOLADAY

As an advertising copywriter, photographer and editor, Chris has had a long career in industries as varied as coffee, sporting goods, specialty groceries and wine. He has also written several nonfiction books with topics that include baseball, auto racing and colonial towns, but all his work has had a focus on Southern history. His work has appeared in *Southern Living*, among other publications, and he has written promotional pieces for the cooking schools of which Marilyn Markel was director. A native of Texas and graduate of the University of North Carolina, he now resides in Durham, North Carolina.